TOKYO

THE CITY AT THE END OF THE WORLD

TOKYO

THE CITY AT THE END OF THE WORLD

Peter Popham

with photographs by
Ben Simmons

KODANSHA INTERNATIONAL LTD.
Tokyo, New York, San Francisco

for my father

Photo and drawing credits: contents page, top, photomontage by Tsunehisa Kimura; p.18, Asahi Shimbun; p. 19, Kyodo News Enterprise Ltd.; pp. 28–29, Kodansha Ltd.; p. 50, Takamitsu Azuma; p. 61, Kisho Kurokawa; p. 80, Mori Building Co., Ltd.; p. 81, Junko Popham; p. 111, Minoru Takeyama; p.118, Arata Isozaki; p. 126, Kokusai Photo; pp. 144–45, Akira Naito (from his book *Katsura*); pp. 148–49, Ch. Hirayama; pp. 150–51, Tokyo National Museum and Yoshio Taniguchi; p. 158, Eijiro Torihata; p. 159, Osamu Murai.

Parts of this book have previously appeared in a different form in the *Mainichi Daily News, Winds, PHP, One Moment of the World, Process Architecture,* and *Asia Magazine.*

Distributed in the United States by Kodansha International/USA Ltd., through Harper & Row, Publishers, Inc., 10 East 53rd Street, New York, New York 10022. Published by Kodansha International Ltd., 12-21, Otowa 2-chome, Bunkyo-ku, Tokyo 112 and Kodansha International/USA Ltd., with offices at 10 East 53rd Street, New York, New York 10022 and The Hearst Building, 5 Third Street, Suite 430, San Francisco, California 94103.

Library of Congress Cataloging in Publication Data

Popham, Peter.
  Tokyo: the city at the end of the world.

  1. Tokyo (Japan)—Description. I. Title.
DS896.35.P66   1985   952'.13504   85-40065
ISBN 0-87011-726-2 (U.S.)
ISBN4-7700-1226-8 (Japan)

CONTENTS

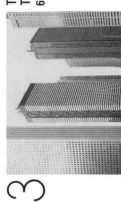

PREFACE

This book is a portrait of contemporary Tokyo: its monuments and shacks, its love hotels and hold-outs, its expressways and village lanes, its still center and its sprawling fringes. I have been bending an ear to this great city, and here is what it had to say to me—about itself and about Japan, but also about the modern city everywhere, and the modern world of which such cities are perhaps the ultimate product.

The book is the outcome of three years' work, but in a way it has been brewing ever since I first arrived in Tokyo over eight years ago. Inevitably it reflects the fact that my roots are in that "stone culture" country, England, different in so many ways from Japan with its "wood culture." But it also reflects the unexpected and paradoxical sense of liberation I have experienced in this paradox-thick megalopolis.

Many people have helped and encouraged me in the project, and I could not have contemplated, let alone completed, it without them. My thanks to them all. It was Deyan Sudjic, then of *Building Design*, now of the *Sunday Times*, who, back in 1979, persuaded me to write some articles about modern Japanese architecture, thereby rekindling an old enthusiasm and focusing my attention on Tokyo. In conversation and through his works and writings, Arata Isozaki sowed seeds which I hope bedded deep enough to have blossomed well. He and his assistant Yoshiko Amiya, who have been kind in many ways, also looked over the text. Takamitsu Azuma read sections of it, too, and answered tricky questions, and he and his wife showed me great hospitality; I have my good friend Hilary McLaine to thank for introducing me to Mr. Azuma and his work. Minoru Takeyama is another accomplished architect whose friendship I appreciate, and whose wisdom has, I profoundly hope, found its way into the book.

Tim Porter said "What about Tokyo?" at the right moment, and worked closely on early ideas for a book about the city. Tom Chapman, editor of JAL's inflight magazine, *Winds*, in a gesture typical of him, gave me the whole English-language section of one issue in which to explore my ideas on the subject, thus bringing me face to face with my own ignorance. Roger Pulvers, editor of the *Mainichi Daily News's* Monday Arts Page persuaded me to write a series of articles on Tokyo's vernacular architecture, entitled *In the Jungle of the City*, which gave me an opportunity to do much necessary research. Yoshinori Sayama, Mike Allen, and Bob Wargo of *PHP Intersect* magazine gave me writing assignments which allowed me to broaden my perspective. Junko, my wife, helped in lots of ways, not least by managing cheerfully when I took weeks off to write the first draft.

Thanks are also due to the following people, all of whom offered valuable assistance of various kinds:

Professor Fumihiko Maki
Professor Hiromichi Ishizuka and Professor Nobuo Marui of Tokyo Municipal University's Toshi Kenkyu Center
Shiomi Sakurai
Naoko Tsunoi
Julia Nolet
Don Morton
Masao Itagaki and Jun'ichi Seto of *Mainichi Shimbun*
Yoshimitsu Isoi of Mori Biru Co., Ltd.
Sai Kumagai of *Mainichi Daily News*
Mama Suzuki
Kazuo Takahashi of *Japan Architect*
Eric Weidermeier
Professor Edward G. Seidensticker
Stephen McLelland

"The history of civilization . . . leaves in architecture its truest, because its most unconscious record."

—Geoffrey Scott, *The Architecture of Humanism*

" . . . To discern, through the walls and towers destined to crumble, the tracery of a pattern so subtle it could escape the termites' gnawing."

—Italo Calvino, *Invisible Cities*

1
THE CITY ABOLISHED

According to the recent prediction of a seismologist, three million people may die in Tokyo's next great earthquake. What will it be like? Having endured any number of smaller ones since coming to live in this city, it's a subject my mind strays to when there is nothing special to occupy it. What would it be like if it were to happen here and now? In this subway train, for example, a quarter of a mile underground at 8:30 in the morning, where we are crammed together like coats in a closet; in this bus in the middle of this jam, surrounded by taxis fueled by LP gas (it goes off like a bomb, they say); or here, fifty-five stories up a West Shinjuku skyscraper? It won't snap, it'll just shake, the wise men say, but what if it shakes me right through the window?

That's the way the murmuring goes. Twenty-eight million people (the population of the Tokyo megalopolis) murmur likewise to themselves every day as their attention drifts away from the matter at hand. Where will I be when it happens? How will I contact the wife? Where would I run if it happened *here*? The big quake is not the sort of thing anyone gets away with forgetting about entirely.

Because even the small ones are bad enough. One's

first quake is unbelievable at the time, unforgettable afterward. It's a new category of experience: the good old earth gone mad! There's the creaking and squawking of timbers, swaying of lamps, tinkling of cups and saucers, but worst is the shuddering of the structure under one's bottom, the powerful awareness that the one element you always take for granted is suddenly quite beyond control.

The first quake is unforgettable, but the second is no better. Japanese are agreed on this: familiarity with earthquakes does not take away their fearfulness. Each small quake means one small one less to go before the next big one. It may even mean the beginning of the end: it may be the forequake, the first gentle lapping of that mighty seismic roller which will bring about, once again, the destruction of the city.

⌗

Against the demonic irrationality of the great quake, Tokyo counterposes the beauty and equally unhuman reliability of the machine.

Every modern city is a machine, but Tokyo is more perfectly so, more elaborately so. One reason is that it *must* be, to survive. With more than twenty-four million people using the city's surface railways and subways every working day, the sort of cancellations and delays that are a fact of life in a city like London would bring paralysis in no time.

Take the Yamanote Line, for example, the railway that circles the central area, passing through half a dozen of the city's major subcenters as it goes. During the morning and evening rush hours, trains leave the line's twenty-nine stations punctually every two to three minutes; at other hours of the day the interval is between four minutes and six. The great majority of trains are about as full as they can get. Once in a blue moon something goes wrong: someone throws himself onto the tracks, or there is a mechanical breakdown. A train is canceled, the gap between trains stretches from three minutes to eight, and suddenly the platform of every major station looks as though a nearby stadium has just disgorged a baseball crowd. In Tokyo there is little margin for error.

But to say that Tokyo works so well because it must is in a sense to dodge the question. It sounds less rational but may be more fruitful to suggest that Tokyo works so well because it wants to, because it enjoys it.

This city is a piece of machinery unrivaled in history for size, complexity, precision; unrivaled for productivity, too, if we measure that in man-miles, sheets of paper, computer printouts, and radio and TV waves. It's of a scale that beggars analogy: far more stupendous than any beehive or termite's colony, any factory.

The ideas and the tools which produced the first archaic prototype of this machine came from the other end of the world, from a culture as unlike Japan's as any the world has seen. Yet somehow the Japanese have made it their own. Charmed throughout their history by the punctiliously correct performance of ritual, they have made of the whole city and its operation a fantastic diurnal ceremony.

In this there is nothing revolutionary; the mechanization which made the modern city possible in the West had, by virtue of its sheer repetitiveness, something ceremonial about it. But in the West it has come to be regarded, except by those who profit from it, as something hateful and oppressive, a mode of work and life which diminishes man's humanity. The indignation and fear behind the images of *Modern Times* and *Metropolis* are still the standard Western reactions to mechanization.

Fascinated rather than fearful, more intrigued than indignant, the Japanese have taken the ceremony of city life to heights of holy precision encountered only in the West's nightmares. In the West the realization that one is a cog in a machine is a source of shame, a reason for rebellion. In Tokyo, when you realize what a damn-near flawless and unprecedentedly magnificent machine you are a perfect cog in, it is, on the contrary, a matter for blissful contemplation:

—the trains, each nearly a quarter of a mile long, each crammed tight, sliding neatly around the Yamanote loop;

—those Victorian reminders: the stationmaster's watch and chain, his flag, his white-gloved salute; the driver's forefinger pointed up the track as he eases out of the station, his ritual declaration, for the hearing of no one in particular, that he is setting off;

—the crowds themselves, immaculate, expression-less, almost odorless, moving through the wickets as fast and impersonally as grain through a hopper;

—all the interconnections: subway to overhead line, expressway to main street, loop line to monorail to jet plane, subway to elevator to elevator to subway, loop line to bullet train; the precise careening in and out and round and round of a thousand thousand beautifully wrapped parcels of dying flesh; the instant apotheosis of that, which is at the same time a stripping away of humanity, a rendering of man into something like the blip of an electrical current. . . .

It's very beautiful and strange, and to appreciate its beauty and strangeness you must leave your surly, frame-breaking Western city and venture to Tokyo, the city where almost nothing ever goes wrong.

And when it *does* go wrong—it does so in no uncer-tain terms. That's quite something to see, too.

⊯

Tokyo has a major earthquake roughly every sixty years. The next one is overdue.

The whole Japanese archipelago is one of the most seismically active areas in the world; long after Western Europe, America, and Australia have been put up in the kiln to bake, Japan is still wet clay in God's hands. Every other year a volcano goes off somewhere; every year earthquake-triggered landslides and tsunami take a few or a few dozen or a few hundred lives.

Tokyo is near one of the areas in Japan where seismic activity is strongest, most persistent, most threatening. When Frank Lloyd Wright stayed in the city during the building of his Imperial Hotel he was awed to discover that the seismometer was never still for a single mo-ment. And on September 1, 1923, the day the hotel op-ened—Wright himself was by then safely back in the States—the biggest quake ever recorded in Tokyo hit his new building such a wallop that the floor of the ban-queting hall instantly dropped two feet. Elsewhere in the city, in the quake and the terrible fire that followed it, close to 140,000 people died.

The area that suffered the worst was, as usual, the proletarian east end of the city, where hundreds of thousands lived tightly packed together on low, marshy land reclaimed from Tokyo Bay, in houses of flimsy wood. Fire raced through that section with astonishing speed. The people fled as fast as they could, but there was nowhere for them to go; Tokyo was not then and is not now a city of open spaces. Some 40,000 gathered next to the garden of a wealthy financier, on open ground near the bay which had been turned into a depot for army clothing. There the flames found them, and roasted the lot.

Only twenty-two years later there was a second disaster of equally vast proportions, this one man-made. During the first three months of 1945, American bombers flew eighty-eight separate missions over Tokyo, during which three-quarters of a million houses were damaged or destroyed and 100,000 people killed. Another 3,000,000 were made homeless. By the time the Americans had finished almost the whole city was a burned-out ruin. Only a few ferroconcrete stumps still stuck up above the cinders.

In the midst of the immaculate machinery of the modern city it's hard to get it into one's head that Tokyo has been more or less erased from the earth not once but twice in the past six and a half decades. And there's every indication that it's going to happen again. Only today's Tokyo is a very different city, and its sufferings will be different, too.

The city that burned in 1923 and 1945 was made almost entirely of wood, and its people and buildings were packed far tighter than those of any Western city. It was so flammable that the people of the east end, the "low city," took it for granted that they would have to build themselves new homes at least once or twice in their lifetimes.

The modern city has much less wood in it. Houses are still built perilously close together, but the old uniformity of wood is broken frequently by larger structures of concrete, even in those parts of the east and which seem to

City in ruins: Tokyo after the earthquake and fire of 1923 . . .

. . . and after the incendiary bombings of 1945.

have been most left behind by the city's postwar success. The flimsy structures thrown up after the war were only good for a few decades, and as their time comes around these shacklike shops and dwellings are replaced by concrete ones. Along the city's hundreds of shopping streets, the old mortar-faced wooden houses are rapidly becoming rarities, as shopkeepers hurry to take advantage of easing height regulations with four- or six- or eight-story ferroconcrete buildings, teetering on the tiny sites that previously looked barely big enough for two-story structures of wood.

Modern Tokyo is thus no longer a tinder box. But its population is quite as dense as it was sixty years ago, and very much larger. Just before the 1923 earthquake the city's population was 2,300,000. Now the population of the city proper is some six times that size, while the population of the megalopolis, including neighboring Yokohama and the suburban areas in the adjacent prefectures, is now, as was mentioned before, about 28,000,000. In 1923 you could have walked from one side of Tokyo to the other in an hour. Now the built-up area of the metropolis covers an area of nearly 2,300 square miles. From north to south and from east to west is a distance of about 40 miles.

The relatively predictable dangers of wood construction have been replaced by others of a far more explosive nature. Main roads are wider than they were forty or sixty years ago, but throughout the daylight hours and into the night they are solid with traffic, which negates their value as avenues of escape and turns them into rivers of gasoline, potential rivers of flame.

The new city has many other perils which had no counterpart in the old one. The huge Tokyo-Yokohama industrial area around the bay is a sea of toxic and flammable chemicals, and also accommodates a nuclear reactor. Dangerous chemicals are also used in the thousands of small-scale manufacturing plants dotted through many residential sections of the city. The charcoal-fired hibachi stoves which started so many fires in 1923 have been replaced by gas mains, and the rupturing of many of the pipes is a foregone conclusion. Ferroconcrete buildings are unlikely to tumble to the ground—though the many cheaply built steel-frame apartment buildings are a real hazard—but anybody unlucky enough to be out in the street will have plenty of falling objects to dodge: concrete utility poles, vending machines, store signs, roof tiles, rooftop water tanks. According to a Tokyo government report, some 15 percent of the buildings higher than two stories will shower objects on the ground.

Gradually a picture of the mayhem of Tokyo's next major earthquake begins to emerge. The imagination's task has been greatly aided by the work of a research group set up at Tokyo Metropolitan University with the specific aim of assessing the likely consequences of such a disaster. The multidisciplinary Disaster Prediction Research Group of the Metropolitan Research Center has been at work since 1976, and in March 1983 it published a report detailing its findings. As the professors are careful to stress, large areas of uncertainty remain, and their predictions are deliberately on the conservative side. They are at pains to avoid being alarmist. They can hardly avoid being alarming.

The great quake of 1923 occurred just before lunchtime. Suppose the next one strikes at the same time? Taking the Metropolitan Research Center's figures on trust, what sort of consequences would it be reasonable to expect?

Suppose you are one of the many millions of people in the city preparing to eat lunch on that day. You are at home in the inner western suburbs—Nakano, let's say, out on the Chuo Railway Line and the No. 7 loop highway, ten or fifteen minutes by train from Shinjuku, the major western subcenter. It's a decent, prosperous part of town where you have a small, stucco-faced wooden house just like your neighbors', with Mediterranean-blue roof tiles. The neighboring houses are all quite close, and the road that winds between them is little better than an alley. But that's one of the charms of the place. It's quiet, cozy, villagelike.

Or you are just leaving your office building in the Ginza, on the eastern side of the Yamanote Line loop, with your colleagues, on the way to a restaurant for lunch. The eight-story building is handsome, clad in polished granite and cream-colored marble. The road outside is six lanes wide, solid with cars as usual. Your favored restaurant is a hundred yards away down a side street.

Or you are just shutting down your machine in a factory in Kawasaki, the industrial city that Tokyo merges with in the south, by the bay. It's not one of those factories staffed by robots. As the somewhat unsuccessful subsidiary of one of the nation's biggest and most conservative concerns, this steel plant is surprisingly labor-intensive. Around it the landscape is rust red in all directions; the only touch of green is provided by a pair of huge gas tanks. With your buddies you move off in the direction of the stand-up noodle shop around the corner.

There is no warning that a quake is coming. Years of effort and billions of yen of research money have failed to yield any reliable method of prediction. Some said catfish would tell you, thrashing anxiously around shortly beforehand; firemen installed them in tanks in their fire stations and the fish sat there stolidly through everything. Undersea sensors were planted deep in trenches off the Pacific coast and yielded plenty of figures but nothing in the way of a warning. Prophets of doom came and went, some, like Masatoshi Sagara (he predicted that Mount Fuji would erupt in 1983), making a fortune in the process, but none getting it right. Scientists keenly observed silk trees, waiting for them to give off abnormally strong electrical charges; non-scientists stared equally keenly at odd-shaped clouds, curious rainbows, flocks of birds, domestic pets. But when the quake comes, no one is ready.

The rumble is heard only a fraction of a second before the first and most devastating shock. There is no time to move, to hit the deck or get under a table. The ground lurches upwards, knocking you straight up in the air. As you fall to the floor, or to the concrete of the street, the shocks continue, wracking the earth with spastic bursts of energy. The noise is deafening now, dense with a thousand different sounds of destruction and dissolution: cracking timbers, smashing glass and crockery, the crumpling of vehicle bodies against concrete, the tumbling of cinderblock walls, the ripping away of balconies, signboards, window-fitted air conditioners, the roar of hardware crashing down into the street. Somewhere at the back of it all is the thin keening of human cries.

Just as on September 1, 1923, everybody is cooking when the quake strikes. It is drummed into the Japanese from childhood that the first thing to do in an earthquake is to turn off gas appliances, and in minor quakes they are quick to do it. A survey conducted after a mild quake in January 1984, for example, revealed that 90 percent of those using gas stoves had turned them off. This time, however, though you know well what you should do, the quake gives you no opportunity. As you lie dazed on the floor, the oil from the tempura frying pan, which the shock upset onto the stove, catches fire, and the flames at once begin leaping up the walls.

The experts of the Metropolitan Research Center reckon that 2,500 to 3,000 fires will start citywide within twenty minutes of the earthquake. Of these, some 300 will turn into major ones.

Over in Ginza, sprawled in the street where you fell, you watch appalled as a massive rooftop air conditioner, weighing perhaps a quarter of a ton, pitches off the still-trembling roof of an older office block across the way, bounces off the entrance porch, buckling it, and stoves in the body of a car gummed up in the traffic. As smaller debris continues to rain down into the street, you and those of your colleagues who can still move crawl for the relative safety of the shopping arcade you were outside when the quake occurred. An explosive *whump* whisks you around: the car hit by the cooling plant is a mess of ragged flames and black smoke, and the drivers of the vehicles behind and in front are desperately trying to put a little distance between it and themselves. To little effect: all six lanes are head-to-tail, and three or four other gasoline fires are burning fiercely nearby, presumably where cars collided, puncturing gas tanks, during the first shock.

The Tokyo Metropolitan Police Department is scrupulous about instructing drivers what they should do in the event of a major earthquake. As soon as cracks appear in the road, they say, drivers should steer their cars into the nearest empty lot, switch off the engine (leaving the key in the ignition), and continue on their way on foot. A 1983 police report laments that only some 23 percent of drivers know that this is what they are supposed to do.

Perhaps more to the point is the fact that, in the case of a real quake, the plan is almost completely unworkable, as drivers, locked in burning traffic, will be unable to take their cars anywhere or do anything at all except get out and run.

. . . Which is what many of Ginza's drivers, aware that shortly the whole road will be awash with flame, have started to do. The shoppers spilling out of the arcade you are attempting to shelter in have the same idea, for the arcade is on fire, too, and they come choking and screaming out of the store's smoky innards. Mowing down the old and feeble they pour down the sidewalk, all in the same direction, the only direction everybody is sure they want to go in, even if they have forgotten everything else: the inner moat of the Imperial Palace—Danger Grade Zero on the metropolitan government's charts.

It's not close; in the best normal conditions, with all the lights on green, it's a brisk ten-minute walk. God knows how long it will take today, or whether even a fraction of these people will get there. But at least it's a rational place to aim for. It's very safe.

Over in suburban Nakano the situation is worse because, just as in the east end in '23 and '45, there is nowhere to go. The intimacy which makes these places worth living in is once again making them eminently suitable for dying in, too.

Remembering the 40,000 burned to death at the army clothing depot in 1923, burned because there was not a sufficiently expansive area of open land for them to flee to, the metropolitan government has designated 134 areas across the city as "safety evacuation areas," with each home, office, and factory in the city allotted to a particular area. These are the places citizens are requested to flee to in the event of a disaster.

Like much else decreed by the city's authorities, this is flawlessly well intentioned but not necessarily very useful. The Tokyo metropolitan government has apparently neither the money nor the willpower to acquire land in use and turn it into open space at points where to do so would be a genuinely useful life-saving measure. Instead they limit themselves to the much simpler and purely bureaucratic task of labeling already existing open spaces, such as they are, "safety evacuation areas," and putting signs on the roads that lead to them. They feel better; the public feels better, too. The underlying problem, however—the fact that the city is drastically short of open space—remains untouched.

As a result, many thousands of people in areas of the city particularly vulnerable to fire disasters are faced with absurdly long and complicated journeys to safety—journeys which, given the likelihood of their encountering en route fires, caved-in roads, maddened and speeding drivers, crowds of people moving in the opposite direction, broken water pipes, and roads blocked by debris, they are fairly unlikely to complete.

That's your problem at home in Nakano. Your house rode the quake well—it pitched about like a little boat in a squall but didn't collapse—but now it's burning to the ground, and with one child strapped to your back and the other in your arms you must run for your life. There's no sense in putting your faith in the Fire Department; even if there were any firetrucks available, none of them is small enough to get down your road. So with neighbors beside you—their houses are burning, too—you hot-foot it down the lane.

... But there is nowhere to go. Your designated evacuation area is a scrap of land around the Nakano Ward Office—but it's on the far side of a broad railway track, and the tunnel under it is blocked with burning vehicles. There's not another accessible patch of green in any direction. Nowhere to go—nothing to do but run to where the flames are not, and pray for hard rain, very soon. For otherwise the city, and Nakano with it, may well be consumed by a firestorm so stupendous that it will make the one of 1923—authoritatively described as "the greatest single conflagration ever ignited on the surface of the globe"—seem no more than the smoldering of autumn leaves.

As for you, down in your factory in Kawasaki, who can tell what your fate was? In the table of likely consequences of an earthquake drawn up by the Metropolitan Research Center, the following hazards are listed under the heading "Factories and Manufacturing":

Collapse of machinery
Breakage of equipment
Fuel spillage
Escape of poison gas
Outbreak of fire—failure to extinguish same
Petrochemical plants? [sic]
Chemical blaze
Nuclear isotope [sic]
Number affected by gas: 91,000 people

In other categories—"Transport," "Shops," "Housing," etc.—the possibility of escape to safety is mentioned, though with the danger of panic beside it in brackets. Under "Factories and Manufacturing," however, the very word "escape" is in brackets, thus:

(Escape)

It's an admirably pithy way of putting it.

#

Tokyo is in many senses well prepared for a great earthquake. The city's people are after all keenly aware that there is one on the way. As a race the Japanese are enormously prudent, and everything that could humanly be done to diminish the destructive potential of the great earthquake—without actually interfering with people's businesses or property—has surely been done.

There are frequent complicated drills, with cohorts of company staffers lined up in protective helmets behind company banners.

There are public loudspeakers, strung, it sometimes seems, from every other tree and utility post in the city, which boom out solemn warnings every time heavy rain or a strong wind threatens. They would surely find plenty to say about a great earthquake.

Everywhere there are conspicuous notices telling people what to do when the quake hits, to turn off the gas and hide under the table. And coming from a tradition of docile submission to authority, people do not question the wisdom of these instructions.

Yet one can't shake the feeling that the supreme futility of most of this will be revealed when the day comes. And beyond that feeling is another one: that somewhere beneath the bureaucratic chatter and the obedience, the Japanese understand the futility quite well themselves.

There, in the dry, carefully considered phrases of the Metropolitan Research Center's report, is the picture of a city helpless to save itself, and reconciled at some quite deep level to destruction and loss of life beyond all but the nuclear nightmares of other cities.

In the immediate aftermath of the earthquake, it is suggested:

Sixty-two thousand two hundred houses will be demolished by the vibrations.

One thousand three hundred cliffs will disintegrate; 190 buildings will be carried away by landslides, another 10,860 houses will be flooded or washed away.

Four point one three square miles of land will be flooded.

Uncontrollable panic will break out in thirty-five separate places.

Two hundred sixteen water mains and 669 gas mains will burst.

Two thousand five hundred to 3,000 fires will break out, 300 of which will become major ones. Within about twenty minutes of the quake the number and intensity of the fires will have got beyond the power of the firefighting services to control; they will have neither enough vehicles nor enough water for the job. The fires will burn on deep into the next day, and 71.9 square miles of land will be burned up. Four hundred seventy-three thousand three hundred houses will be destroyed.

By the time the disaster services get around to counting—sometime during the next day, it's suggested—there will be 35,700 people dead and 63,000 injured. Some 3,499,200 people will be rendered homeless.

This is the rational, considered, deliberately conservative assessment of what the future holds for Tokyo, the world's largest city. When it was published in spring 1983 there was no outcry, no flood of demands for job transfers, no rush of city property onto the market. "Our report was well received in the press," says Professor Hiromichi Ishizuka, chairman of the Metropolitan Research Center. There were finger-wagging editorials, complaints of ill-preparedness, then the small, dutiful commotion died down.

Why does it not upset the people more, the fact that they might any day be roasted alive, gassed to death, buried in a landslide or in the wreckage of their own houses? It's one of modern Tokyo's enduring mysteries. One answer may be that, far from being dull to the

Earthquake drill in central Tokyo.

dangers, acute awareness of them gives Tokyo people's lives tone and brio; that foreknowledge of disaster does in fact, as it was claimed to do, "concentrate the mind wonderfully." The satisfaction of being a cog in the most elaborate and well-oiled machine in the history of the world is given almost an erotic twist by the knowledge that the machine is poised over an abyss.

In his novel *Invisible Cities*, Italo Calvino conceives of just such a place. "Now I will tell how Octavia, the spider-web city, is made," declares Marco Polo to Kublai Khan.

There is a precipice between two steep mountains: the city is over the void, bound to the two crests with ropes and chains and catwalks. You walk on the little wooden ties, careful not to set your foot in the open spaces, or you cling to the hempen strands. Below there is nothing for hundreds and hundreds of feet: a few clouds glide past; farther down you can glimpse the chasm's bed.

This is the foundation of the city: a net which serves as passage and as support. All the rest, instead of rising up, is hung below: rope ladders, hammocks, houses made like sacks, clothes hangers. . . .

Suspended over the abyss, the life of Octavia's inhabitants is less uncertain than in other cities. They know the net will only last so long.

⊞

The world has lived in the shadow of nuclear weapons for decades now. But though the nature of the weapons has changed, and their number has multiplied, the image of nuclear disaster which affects us most strongly is the same as that by which their existence was first brought to our attention. Whether the perceived danger is a "limited" nuclear war or an all-out intercontinental exchange, it's the prospect of the city abolished—flattened, burned, irradiated—which really frightens us.

The power of Jonathan Schell's *The Fate of the Earth* came from his cool, analytical description of the different ways New York would be turned inside out by a nuclear attack. The fascination of General Sir John Hackett's otherwise dryly strategic *The Third World War* was that it posited, as the war's climactic event, the annihilation of Birmingham, England. Similarly, the American TV film *The Day After* would have been much less gripping if the only places destroyed had been missile silos, or if the victimized city had been strange or far away. Instead what was blown to bits was a real American city, Lawrence, Kansas, as banal and ordinary and familiar as your big sister, and a hundred million viewers stayed tuned.

For to destroy the city is the forbidden thing. Man can lay nature waste and we wring our hands and condemn it, but it doesn't reach our deepest place—because this is what man has always done, just to survive. Man can kill other men, but their young sons are already growing. The city, however, is man's greatest work: hacked out of the wilderness, put painfully in place stone by stone, the concrete outcome of a million different flashes of inspiration and curlicues of ingenuity, a thousand million man-hours of sweated labor. To wipe it away is to wipe out what man has made of himself. So we read about or watch its fictional abolition with fascination, perhaps even with a sort of vicarious sadistic pleasure. But when we think of the same thing happening to our own city, in real life, the emotion is blank dread.

Of all cities, Hiroshima remains the one most closely bound up with the bomb, and forty years after they began to disappear under new construction, that city's charred, empty acres remain the most vivid image of nuclear destruction we know. Yet the destruction suffered by Hiroshima was not unique; nor, except in details, were its stigmata peculiarly nuclear ones. Those details, the stone and steel melted by the intense heat, the shadows of burned individuals left printed on stone, were shockingly novel enough. But the image of actual annihilation—the plain of ashes, senselessly cut up into empty blocks by empty streets—was a result not so much of the power of the bomb as of the combustibility of the city on which it was dropped.

What was unique about Hiroshima was that its destruction was brought about by a single device. Tokyo received the bombs of 4,870 U.S. planes before it was decided that no further damage could be done. But the combustibility of the capital, built, with the exception of the stone and brick business district at the center, of the same flimsy materials as Hiroshima, ensured that when the bombs had done their work all that was left of the city were cinder fields, just like Hiroshima's. The majority of Japan's cities suffered in the same way. Large areas of almost all of them, with the exception of Kyoto, were completely erased.

Neither the cities of the West nor those of modern Japan will ever burn as clean or flat as Japan's wooden cities did during the last war, no matter how many earthquakes clobber them or how many nuclear devices rain down. Nevertheless, that is the image of nuclear annihilation at the back of our own nuclear fears. And the memory of that great incineration, shared as it is by millions, remains a potent force in contemporary Japan.

It's not, as you might expect, a totally black, nihilistic force either. Those who were children or adolescents during the war, and watched their cities burn, in particular seem to feel deeply ambivalent about the experience.

Tsunehisa Kimura is an artist in Tokyo, a fabricator of extraordinary and apocalyptic photomontages. He was born and raised in Osaka, the nation's second city (third now in population after Yokohama), and was a design student there in the last year of the war. Tokyo is a patchwork of hills and flatlands. Osaka, however, like Hiroshima, is located on a flat flood plain, and in 1945 it was densely built up over an area of many square miles. The usual tightly packed wooden houses were interspersed here and there by factory chimneys and larger structures of concrete or stone.

Kimura remembers the night the B-29s came well. The terror has gone now, or at least he is successful in keeping it out of his voice. What remain are visions of uncanny beauty.

"Like other towns, every section of Osaka had a fire tower raised high above the rooftops, with a bell in it," he told me in a coffee shop near his Tokyo studio. "The B-29s came flying over the city in a circular formation. Each plane dropped its bombs—incendiary bombs I suppose—in a bundle, then the bundle broke up and the individual bombs fanned out, and each bomb had a flame coming out of it. So all across the sky there were these points of flame drifting down.

"As the planes flew over and dropped their bombs the bells in the fire towers began ringing, one after another, till the sound seemed to be coming from all directions. After they had passed over the city once, they came back and did it again and again, crisscrossing methodically to make sure the whole place was burning well. By the time they had finished there were high flames wherever you looked. Everything was burning. Our house was near a river. It caught fire so we got out and ran to the riverbank. The only thing we managed to salvage was my elder brother's large electric gramophone. My mother staggered out with that, leaving everything else behind.

"The planes came over around 11 P.M. and the fires burned from then till 3 A.M., when a heavy black rain, precipitated by the intense heat over the city, began to fall and put them out. And in the morning the sun came up and it was a beautiful day. I'll never forget the way the city looked then.

"There was nothing left standing at all in any direction except a few chimneys and concrete shells. For the rest, the city was now as flat as this table. There were only a few indications that just yesterday the whole plain had been covered with houses. One was the blackened corpses to be seen here and there. Another was the heaps of charcoal. During the war everybody was illegally buying and hoarding fuel, keeping it a dark secret from their neighbors. Now on the burned-out site of every house was to be seen a little heap of charcoal. It was quite funny.

"The other thing was the pipes everywhere, stuck up two or three feet above the ground. They were still in place, and water was pouring out of them onto the ground. And as I say, it was a lovely day, the sun was shining, and all over the city—black cinders, nothing standing for miles—were hundreds of jets of water, hundreds of little rainbows."

This was it! Here was Buddhism's "world of empty oneness"! The highest expressions of Japanese culture centuries before had been posited on direct experience of that world, of the silence at the heart of the noisiest crowd, the nothingness at the heart of all phenomena. And suddenly, here it was . . . rendered magically visible! Terror and elation, elation and terror, circled round and round, snapping by turns at the heart.

There was everything to be done. All the walls hemming in aspiration were gone. Yet before one's eyes were miles and miles of evidence of the futility of whatever might be attempted, intimations of the blackened ashes to which one's own exertions, too, would someday be reduced.

In the West we look at those old black-and-white

aerial photos of Hiroshima's cinder plains and feel only dread. Those, in Hiroshima, Osaka, and Tokyo, who have been awake and wide-eyed through the whole perform- ance, feel a much more complicated emotion.

⧺

In Hiroshima, in Dresden, in Coventry, fragments of the wartime devastation have been preserved as reminders of what happened. There's nothing like that in Tokyo; the people seem too busy to bother. Nor is there much evidence of real, tough-minded preparation—in the form, perhaps, of mass shelters, wide firebreaks, or strategically created open spaces—for the destruction by earthquake and fire that is to come. Tokyo seems to be a city with neither memory nor imagination, living, like an idiot or an animal, only in and for the present.

Yet beneath the idiot mask, Tokyo is wiser than other cities. The awareness that it is perched between disas- ters, that its time isn't long, permeates all its works. This knowledge gives to the city's life a unique ener- gy and concentration. It tacks on to everything the city does a long black shadow of futility. Sometimes it makes this most palpable, most literally concrete of cities, seem as insubstantial as a cloud.

New York, Birmingham, and Lawrence, Kansas, shake in their boots over what the future may bring. Tokyo knows. That's why it is the city of the end of the twen- tieth century, par excellence.

"I'm very interested in ruins," said the architect Arata Isozaki, in a 1984 interview in the Japanese edition of Playboy. "For me, the moment of ecstasy is when everything that is built vanishes in a catastrophe. Yet at the same time I'm related to this society as an architect who is expected to create proper buildings. So there is a deep contradiction between my inner feelings and my occupation.

"If I were to leave my imprint on the earth I would choose it to be, not in the form of a solid, monumental building—that is the way of the past—but in the ruins of something that has been blasted to pieces and blotted out. That's the sort of monument I would choose."

2
THE VILLAGE DREAM

I am sitting in a coffee shop called Mon Chardon on Kira Dori, "Kira Avenue," one of the smartest young parts of western central Tokyo, not only hearing but vibrating to the black discofunk music which is thumping out of the loudspeakers, because what's sold here is "body sonic coffee," which means the chairs are wired up to the sound system. And I'm looking out of the window on this blowy spring afternoon, my guts bumping back and forth, when the man I interviewed near here three or four days previously comes down the steps of his house on the opposite side of the road, and begins walking in the direction of his studio.

I have to follow him. I want to see where he goes, what he passes through, where he ends up.

The man's name is Takamitsu Azuma. He's one of Tokyo's greatest fans.

Azuma is an architect. Like the photomontage artist Kimura, he was born and raised in Osaka, but for most of the war was an evacuee in the countryside. When he returned to Osaka, his city's new deathscape had an odd effect on him. "I went back on the day the war ended," he had told me as we waited to cross a busy road. "Here and there the ruins were still smoking. 'This is the beginning of our postwar life," I remember thinking. The whole place was burned up. It looked to me like a fantastic landscape out of my dreams, a place full of treasure, full of fascinating things. My decision to become an architect was greatly influenced by that sight . . . by the feeling that from these meaningless bits of debris something marvelous could materialize. Many of the children who saw scenes like this had dreams about them later . . . enjoyable dreams! And it's our generation which is making the present age."

Like the great majority of Japan's talented and ambitious, Azuma has made his base in Tokyo. Tokyo is both the forge and the backdrop for that "something marvelous" he envisioned at the war's end—Tokyo, the seismic graveyard! He's got nearly as close to its doomed heart as he can. He's dug himself in there.

While others were moving out to the relative safety and cheapness and expansiveness of the new suburbs, Azuma bought the biggest plot of inner-city land he could afford—big enough, you would judge, to put a decent-sized tool shed on—and built a family house on it. He's been there nearly twenty years, and he exudes contentment. Nobody has a good word to say for Tokyo's environment. Around the world its photochemical smogs, traffic jams, and insane congestion are well known. Yet here at the heart of it is a really happy man. And happy not only for himself; Tokyo, he believes, is happy with him. "City planners criticize Tokyo a lot and worry about it," he says. "Some say it is so dangerous we need to tear it down and redevelop it all over again. I don't share that view at all. I much prefer it the way it is."

Azuma's view implies that there are things in the city worth holding on to, things that it is doing right. Yet many who have visited Tokyo would have trouble making a list of them; many would hesitate to say that the city was even habitable. My own first impression of Tokyo is etched deeply in my memory. When I arrived in 1977, the principal port of entry was still Haneda, built on reclaimed land jutting out into Tokyo Bay. Instead of weather that day there was a sort of blinding, bronze-colored haze. The airport buildings were of dirty concrete and unremarkable. The first Japanese thing I saw was an old lady sitting on a leatherette bench with her feet tucked under her bottom. Strange . . .

The woman who had promised to employ me collected me in her car and told me that I had missed the annual cherry blossoms but was in time for the annual transport strike. We left the airport and got onto the expressway. It was elevated all the way into town. This afforded us a good prospect.

For obvious reasons, few big airports are located in the midst of beautiful scenery (Narita, Tokyo's new one way out to the northeast, is a weird exception), but the harsh jumble that lines the route from Haneda to the city center struck me at once as something rather special. I saw blocks of flats, factories, a horse-racing track, a sewage farm, a black-tiled temple hemmed about by graves, a rusting scrapyard, warehouses hung with company names—SANYO, SONY, NEC—high of-fice blocks of crude concrete rammed right up against a section of old brown wooden houses packed together as tight as they could go. It was a mess of highly assertive and wildly incongruous elements, all abutting each other without a hint of compromise or deference, and with no trace of organization. Everything seemed in flux: little old pitched-roof wooden structures were smothered by huge modern rectilinear façades, roof-tops sprouted annexes of corrugated PVC, a monorail track popped out of what looked like a lump of solid building.

My future employer asked me about the weather in England, the trip over, whether I had slept . . . .

The whole thing got more intense the closer we got to the center. The overwhelming impression was of a city in the grips of a cruel and desperate struggle to survive. Every narrow plot was filled to bursting, and the complete lack of harmony between neighboring buildings in size, color, or style suggested antagonistic species of animals, enraged by their enforced proximity and trying out every trick of aggression and repulsion in their reper-tory—turning purple all over, baring wicked teeth or an ugly rump, spewing out fumes. . . . Here were the old ones, shabby old boxes, crumbling away; here were the new ones, lacking any sign that things might get easier or more elegant from now on, baldly utilitarian, or, if more than that, as angry and assertive-looking as they could cheaply be made.

When night fell I found myself in Shinjuku, alone in the thick of the neon forest, swept along by impossibly dense throngs of people down lurid little lanes sticky with smells of barbecued offal, and other smells of drains backing up and raw sewage. I pulled free of the crowd, crossed a footbridge, and wandered into a skyscraper and took the elevator to the top and found—too numb by now to feel surprised—that the city and its lights went on forever, as far as the eye could see.

There is a film, *Blade Runner*, set in a Los Angeles thirty-five years hence where it never stops raining and where the argot is a mix of English, Spanish, and Japanese, which captures this face of Tokyo brilliantly. The city in the film, where mysterious balls of gasoline flame billow up towards a poisoned sky, is so bleakly

Tokyo's contemporary skyline.

devoted to satisfying the fancies of massman that everything else—nature, space, air—has had to be banished; a city of decadent beauty, at the far edge of ecological exhaustion.

This is the face central Tokyo shows to the new arrival, and there was plenty of the same sort of thing to be seen from my coffee shop in Kira Dori. The usual concrete utility poles, superfat and conspicuous, measured out both sides of the street. Steel crashguards with a fluorescent stripe lined the narrow sidewalks. Beyond was the an-aesthetic jumble of concrete boxes, some faced with lavatorial ceramic tile. The ragged skyline was about four stories high. Tokyo's modern idea of decorativeness was in evidence at the top of the lamp standards: instead of a functional-looking lamp, each was adorned, at the end of a wavy bit of wrought iron, with two things like flying saucers, decked out with red plastic trim.

As I paid for my coffee, Azuma passed on the opposite side of the road, a plump, comfortable-looking figure approaching fifty in a dark blue shirt, diagonally striped tie, and blazer. He must have just had his lunch; now he was on his way back to work. From his right hand dangled a plastic carrier bag, in his left he held a paperback which he read as he walked along. "It's only five minutes from the house to my studio," he had remarked just before we parted on that previous occasion, "but I have some of my best ideas on those walks."

I left the shop and got on to his tail.

Down the road the architectural jumble continued, but as we approached a major intersection there was a sudden jump in scale. This was Aoyama Dori. "Aoyama Avenue," a major east-west artery of the city with ten lanes of fast-moving traffic. The shopping complex at one corner of the crossing was eleven stories high. The other buildings lining the main road were also high, solid, glossily finished. They belonged on that artery, which is also the fashionable center of Aoyama, one of the capital's most chic and expensive shopping areas. Close to the crossing were a multistory supermarket, a pompous-looking credit bank. There was the Japan Traditional Craft Center, encased in mirror-glass. Among the blue-suited company men and the bourgeois-looking ladies out shopping was a gaggle of Caucasian models.

Azuma crossed over, turned right along the main road, and kept walking. He was still reading.

Then two hundred yards further on (he had just gone past the Aix-en-Provence Gourmet Vegetable and Fruit Store and Gooseberry Coffee Shop), he abruptly turned left, and I nearly lost him. He turned down a snicket so narrow you might have taken it for a private drive. It was about nine feet wide. On either side, a white line painted on the road eighteen inches in from the edge showed where to walk.

Ten lanes had shrunk in one movement to less than ten feet. In the space of a couple of yards we had passed from a place that felt like a big city to a place that had the scale of a village and the pace and activity of a small town.

The shops on either side of this lane were small-town ones, modest and respectable, useful, and a little old-fashioned: a school-uniform outfitter, a liquor store, a calligraphy school, a dry cleaner's, a sweet shop, a stationery shop, a cake and cookie shop, a real estate agent's, a drug store, a small Chinese restaurant, a lumber yard. It was Japanese Penny Lane. The granny who ran the drug store was having a good jaw with a customer. A housewife with a baby on her back was taking her dog for a walk, carrying trowel and tissues to scoop up the poop. Small schoolboys with bulky leather satchels and caps with shiny peaks were buying ice creams. A college-student type was smiling and bowing her way out of the real estate agent's. The cook at the Chinese restaurant came out the back, wiped his hands on the rag around his neck, and lit a cigarette.

And in between the restaurant and the lumber yard Azuma turned right, and the scene changed again.

Now he had brought me to the innermost core. This lane was even narrower: barely eight feet. Here there were no shops, and no vehicles but bikes. On both sides there were two-story stucco houses and apartments behind tiny gardens behind concrete-block walls. There

Takamitsu Azuma's studio, where the *shaga* flowers bloom and the birds twitter.

was nobody around. The humble, bell-like white irises the Japanese call *shaga* were in bloom and you could hear birds twittering. It was really quiet.

Fifty yards down, Azuma closed his book and went into his studio. Right outside, a big cherry tree was beginning to drop its blossoms on the ground.

⨎

You do not have to think that Tokyo is beautiful to concede that it is in many parts exceedingly wholesome. In *The Death and Life of Great American Cities*, Jane Jacobs identifies a quality of the section of Greenwich Village where she was living at the time which made it, she realized, a safe and wholesome part of the city: it was full of watchers. Because of the stores on the street, and the rich mix of people using it, from morning till late in the evening there were always responsible adults keeping a quiet, unemphatic eye on things. They

didn't have to police the place; their mere presence was enough to keep the peace, and also, as she lyrically evokes, to keep the life of the area flowing—the gossip, the news, the goods:

Under the seeming disorder of the old city, wherever the old city is working successfully, is a marvelous order for maintaining the safety of the streets and the freedom of the city. It is a complex order. Its essence is intricacy of sidewalk use, bringing with it a constant succession of eyes. This order is all composed of movement and change, and although it is life, not art, we may fancifully call it the art form of the city and liken it to the dance ... to an intricate ballet in which the individual dancers and ensembles all have distinctive parts which miraculously reinforce each other and compose an orderly whole. . . .

When I get home after work, the ballet is reaching its crescendo. This is the time of roller skates and stilts and tricycles, and games in the lee of the stoop with bottle tops and plastic cowboys; this is the time of bundles and packages, zigzagging from the drugstore to the fruit stand and back over to the butcher's; this is the time when teenagers, all dressed up, are pausing to ask if their slips show or their collars look right; this is the time when beautiful girls get out of M.G.s; this is the time when the fire engines go through; this is the time when anybody you know around Hudson Street will go by.

The liveliness of the street of shops on the way to Azuma's studio has a similar quality. The vibration given off by a living community like this is quite tangible. It binds shopkeeper to customer, neighbor to neighbor, the oldest to the youngest, it binds all the different trades that keep the place alive and functioning. In Japan the principal symbol of this vibrant sense of the community's wholeness is the *matsuri*, the local festival. As the *mikoshi*, the portable shrine containing the local tutelary divinity, is carried round and round the neighborhood by the local shopkeepers and artisans, it delineates the community's territory, and binds its members closer than ever through the fellowship of sweated exertion.

On the road to Azuma's studio, and in the area immediately around it, there is not a single scrap of public open space. Again, Jane Jacobs would nod her head in appreciative understanding. Conventional Western planning theory says that cities need the "lungs" of public parkland not only for their oxygen but simply to stay sane. No, says Jacobs; parks *can* be wholesome and life-giving, but equally they can turn into evil places. If unwatched or underused, they can cause communities far more harm than good. Tokyo bears her out. To be sure, nobody would actually *protest* if the city had more parks, but it gets by remarkably sanely as it is. Tokyo has one-eighth the parkland per capita of New York and one-fourteenth that of London, but a crime rate which is only a fraction of that of either city.

On this reading, then, the small-town community feeling of back-street Aoyama begins to look very much like that of back-street Greenwich Village, with a couple of picturesque Oriental features thrown in for good

Sanja Matsuri in Asakusa, one of Tokyo's grandest street festivals. ▼

measure. And as far as the street of shops goes this is surely true: allowing for different customs and accents and odors, community feelings of this type can probably be found all over the world.

It's when we consider what is at either end of the street of shops that it begins to look rather different.

I have already mentioned the suddenness with which the metropolitan scale of Aoyama Dori shrank to the scale of a small town. In that sudden switch there was nothing pleasing or neatly contrived. It was more like a conjuring trick, a vanishing trick. It was as if the two elements, small-town Aoyama and great-metropolis Aoyama, had reached an agreement that each should carry on as if the other did not exist. You could cover the distance between them in a split second, but each time it was like crossing into a different dimension, stepping into a time warp.

This is the way the community reacts to the threat of fragmentation implicit in the extra-human scale of modern technology—in particular the threat posed by multistory concrete buildings and multilane expressways. It does not permit itself to be decimated. Sheltering behind a protective layer that is actually constructed from the elements that would obliterate it—ferroconcrete and plate glass—it survives.

Similar communities can be found in many parts of Tokyo. Perhaps their survival is due to chance; perhaps it is simply that so far the speculators have not worked their way around to them. Yet to this observer they seem endowed with a type of solidarity, and an instinct for survival, rarely encountered in working-class sections of Western cities. This instinct tells them that merely to resist—stubbornly to contend every inch—is futile. The result is extinction. The trick is to yield what must be yielded—to yield what the stronger is determined to seize—and to hold fast only to what is essential. This part of Aoyama yielded the medieval quietness and smallness of scale of the streets that encircled it. It preserved its living heart.

Small-town sections of some other Japanese cities have achieved the same thing. First-time visitors to "Kyoto the Beautiful" are often appalled by what they see, for the modern rind of that city is quite as cheesy as Tokyo's. But as another architect, Minoru Takeyama, has explained, the broad streets of Kyoto with their vulgar concrete buildings function as a barricade behind which this most traditional of cities goes placidly about its old ways.

This is easier to see in Kyoto because of the city's clearer design. Kyoto became the nation's capital in the eighth century when the influence of T'ang China on Japan was at its height, and the city is laid out in the regular grid form favored by the Chinese. But this never became the Japanese way; the experiment was never repeated on anything like as grand a scale. Chinese geomantic considerations were taken into account at the founding of Edo, the city which was to grow into Tokyo, in 1590, but no attempt was made to impose an abstract pattern on it in the Chinese manner. The crazy convolutions which make Tokyo such a notoriously easy city to get lost in were there in embryo from the outset.

And these characteristic convolutions are the source of another peculiarity of Azuma's neighborhood.

Kyoto, like Chinese and Western cities, is founded on a system of roads. Tokyo is like a negative print of that: it is founded on a system of quarters or blocks.

Even when a Western city is not cut up according to a regular grid like Kyoto's or New York's, the road, and that pattern of movement through the city which the road both facilitates and symbolizes, is still the most basic thing about it. Every house opens on to a road; and the fact that a road needs to be approximately straight to be of much use naturally results in rows of houses lined up alongside each other in roughly straight lines.

Tokyo's residential neighborhoods are constructed on altogether different principles. Access roads of course they have, but the sort of residential roads which have houses slotted into their margins are rare. Instead of such a network, the neighborhood is composed of roughly oblong plots of property nested tightly together, around whose boundaries narrow lanes fiddle a way as best they can.

This different principle of construction has various

consequences. One is that the lanes of the city do not feel public in the way the roads of the Western city do. Another is that, with the exception of a handful of major arteries, the Western idea of naming streets and numbering houses has never caught on. Streets seem to have too little significance in the Japanese urban scheme of things to warrant the prestige that names confer. Houses these days are numbered, but as they are not lined up in rows, there is no logical order for the numbering to follow. When the house-numbering system was first introduced a century ago, householders asked the authorities for whatever number took their fancy. The present-day system is only marginally more helpful.

This focus on the plot rather than the road also has an important consequence for the quality of Tokyo's inner-city environment.

Roads, whether they run straight or curve, tend to create a degree of continuity and uniformity along their length. It is through the network of roads that the big-city mood is spread through a city's length and breadth.

In Aoyama Dori, Tokyo has a magnificent road, which carries the big-city mood with it from end to end. But it fails to create the sort of network any Western city has, because any turning off may, like Azuma's, be less than ten feet wide. The big-city mood is too wide to squeeze down it. And along the narrow and crooked lanes within, quite different rhythms persist unmolested.

Lacking the structure of straight, intersecting lines that roads impose, Azuma's Aoyama assumes a different form, something closer to a spiral, or several circles, each nesting inside a larger one. The image that comes to mind is that of a nut or an egg. On the outside is the high concrete of Aoyama Dori—the hard shell. Within is the street of shops, but in a sense this is no more than the space inside the walnut shell or the white of the egg. It's within this, cradled by it, that is to be found the heart of the matter, the egg's yolk, the kernel. The shopping street's deepest, most basic function is to serve as a mediating space between the roaring, ten-lane city and that soft yolk, the community's kernel, the little lane Azuma turned down last of all.

Tokyo wraps up its private heart as painstakingly as if it were a fragile gift. Inside, in the middle, the *shaga* flowers bloom and the birds twitter. Other cities have their quiet streets, their oases of tranquillity, but they are usually quiet because they are peripheral. Tokyo's quiet parts are quiet because they are central. It's an odd, important difference.

#

Azuma's own house is not wooden, nor is it embowered by Tokyo in the way his studio is. As an Osaka man and a white-collar professional, Azuma is doubly an outsider in those intimate lanes. Sense of class is relatively weak in Japan, but a sense of difference remains. Azuma may own that he loves the place, but he will never *belong* as he would if he had been born there.

He lives only five minutes away, but he's out on a fringe. His house is right opposite the body-sonic coffee shop I was vibrating in when this chapter opened.

The four-lane street which that café and his house face on to is a new one, carved through by the metropolitan government in preparation for 1964's Olympic Games, cutting a slice out of the old community, throwing the old nest-egg geometry of the place into confusion. Now the new road drives one way and all the old lanes butt into it at awkward angles, still flaunting their old community life like the waving segments of a worm that won't admit it's been cut into bits. And along that raw edge have sprung up, like scar tissue, body-sonic coffee shops, madly cool or madly mad boutiques, small galleries, smart beauty shops, and Mr. Azuma's house.

He's perched on the hurting edge. The front of his house is aligned with the main road. The sides line up with the old lane that was here from before, which means the angle between the house's front and side walls has to be about forty-five degrees. Whatever the structural cost, he's determined to relate to both old and new, to face both ways. It's a classic liberal posture.

The angle of the walls is not the only thing that's funny about his house. The plot of land he managed to buy back in the mid-'60s was only 215 square feet in area. But as he was a married man with a young child, what

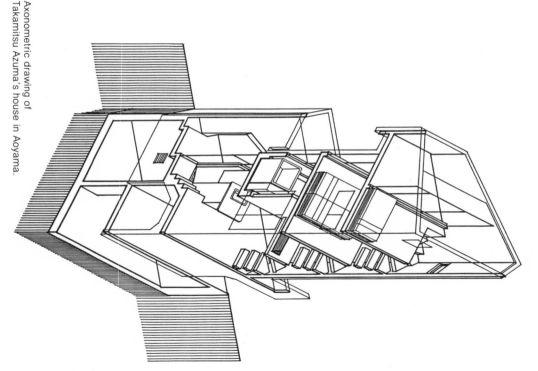

Axonometric drawing of
Takamitsu Azuma's house in Aoyama.

he needed was a family house. And a house fit for a family is what he built.

The result was so extraordinary that almost since the
day it was completed Mrs. Azuma has been kept busy
dishing out tea and cake to the legions of architectural
students tramping through it.

With a plot as narrow as this, what Azuma had to do
was go up. The house is a thin tower, with four floors
above the ground and one below. The only door in the
house is the front one; other than that there are neither

solid doors nor anything in the way of permanent room dividers, from the bottom of the house to the top.

Stepping up from the *genkan*, the place for removing shoes, we arrive in the combined kitchen, dining room, and living room. The house's internal area is about 118 square feet, or seven tatami mats, pretty small even for a traditional tatami-floored Japanese room with nothing in the way of furniture but a low table and a decorative vase with a branch in it. This room, however, is crowded. There's an oven, a fridge, food-preparing surfaces, and a counter separating the kitchen area from the rest (which also functions as the family dinner table), and around the walls there are Western-style chairs. The area of open space is thus reduced to a corridor about a foot wide—fine unless two people try to stand up and move around at the same time. The ceiling over this area is double-height, its volume emphasized by a long, thin, angular paper-covered lampshade, so at least you get the feeling that there is air to breathe.

Concrete steps projecting from the wall carry us up to the next floor, even smaller than the one below, thanks to the ground floor's double-height ceiling. Here Mr. Azuma can keep an eye on the main street's comings and goings while he bathes. Bath and toilet are both closeted behind curtains.

The top two floors are bedrooms, and indeed there is room for little else once the beds are in. At the top we break in on Rie, the Azumas' twenty-five-year-old daughter, cramming for the exams that, if she passes, will take her to Cornell University as a postgraduate architecture student. "No, I don't find it a difficult house to live in," she tells us, "but then I've been here since I was six."

With its tiny dimensions, continuous spaces, and absence of permanent dividers, the Azumas' is an authentic Japanese house; the main divergence from the norm is that it goes upwards rather than sideways. "When foreign architects came to look at it during the '60s," Mr. Azuma told me, "they always asked, 'Why don't you use tatami?' Recently people don't ask that. They seem to have understood that we Japanese have been learning to adapt to Western ways ever since the Meiji period, and that for us there can be no going back.

That's why my house is designed in Western style.

"But even though there is no tatami, I find that I have designed this house with what I call 'tatami-mind.' What that means is that we don't erect solid walls between rooms. The family is able to live with different spaces which are separated merely by a curtain, shoji, or suchlike. As my house is on a very tiny site, there is only one room on each floor, but top and bottom are all connected. It might be fair to say that the reason we can live contentedly like this is because we are Japanese."

When the house was first built, all the neighboring ones were traditional two-story structures of wood. With its naked concrete and rakish outline, the new house must have looked astoundingly modern. Nowadays its neighbors along the street dwarf it with their own barbaric versions of the concrete idiom, and it looks a little seedy, but there's still something extraordinary and eye-popping about it.

It's not essentially something architectural. What it is, rather, is Mr. Azuma's cussedness and obstinacy in insisting on living in a place like this in a way that cuts so directly against the grain of the times. His house is a beacon of individualistic stubbornness—and that in a culture where individualism is a dirty word routinely confused with simple egotism.

Where he *ought* to be, of course, where all his conforming contemporaries are, is in the suburbs. In Tokyo there are plenty to choose from.

The way a city turns into a megalopolis is primarily through the accretion of suburbs. In most cases accretion is made possible by the development of suburban railways which operate fast, frequently, and cheaply enough to allow the people who work in the city's central institutions to commute. This was the way London and New York swelled to megalopolis size between the turn of the century and the Second World War. And it was through a similarly dense network of private railways that the Los Angeles megalopolis came about. They later dried up and were replaced by the freeways which have become the city's symbol, but the achievement of knitting the city's far-flung parts together was theirs.

The same is true of Tokyo, with the difference that the process is still going on. Tokyo has been expanding for a century, but all the most vigorous growth has occurred since the war. In 1910 very little of the city protruded more than six miles beyond the center. By 1932 the six-mile zone was pretty thoroughly built up, and a few ragged corners poked beyond ten miles. By 1960, however, the outer limit had jumped to eighteen miles. By 1975, after more than a decade of unprecedentedly rapid economic growth, much the greater part of the area lying within an eighteen-mile radius of the center had been completely developed, and in the west and southwest the built-up zone continued for dozens of miles more. And while the outer limits are still being explored, consolidation of the area within those limits goes on all the time. Privately developed "bed towns" are continually springing up, with shopping centers and massive slabs of highrise apartments, in places where only a handful of years ago there was nothing to be seen but paddy fields.

⨲

The preferred location for the new bed town is close to a railway station on a private line. While the network of Japan's nationalized system, JNR, has changed little since the war (except for the addition of the Shinkansen or high-speed "bullet train" lines), the private network, comprising more than half a dozen companies, has grown with incredible vigor.

Their development constitutes a total and superbly profitable package. At one of Tokyo's subcenters, which will also be a major interchange station on the Yamanote Line that encircles the city—Shibuya and Ikebukuro are two of the best examples—the firm builds a department store (depato): the Tokyu firm in Shibuya, for example, or Seibu in Ikebukuro. To bring the shoppers to the store the firm next shoots out a private railway line from the front steps of the depato deep into the boondocks. Soon newcomers to the capital are flocking to live along this handy new line, and to accommodate them the firm sets up a real-estate division, and goes into the business of building bed towns.

It's a marvelous, self-generating enterprise which has made Japan's department stores, the queen bees at the heart of the system, among the biggest and by far the most flourishing and dynamic in the world. Seibu's Ikebukuro store, for example, the largest in Japan, has floors of gourmet foods, a champagne bar, an in-store community college, a "creative forum" for hobbyists, a four-floor sports hall, a 400,000-volume bookstore, and a museum, in addition to all the things one would expect. The prosperity of stores like Seibu, based on the flow of money and commodities up and down the private railway lines, is one of the biggest factors behind the amazing efflorescence of Japanese fashion over the past fifteen years, a trend which such stores have nurtured carefully.

Meanwhile the blocking-in of farmland with suburbs continues remorselessly, dependent only on the continuing growth of the economy and of employment opportunities within it and the willingness of the commuter to put up with traveling an hour, an hour and a half, or two hours to work and back, often standing the whole way, five or six days a week. But if the economy can keep it up, the commuter can be counted on to do his bit: power of endurance is one of the national characteristics of which the Japanese are proudest. Besides, everyone does it so it must be OK. Takamitsu Azuma wakes up in the morning and walks to work in five minutes, reading a book. But he's odd, he's weird.

One of the results of the near-simultaneous development of dozens of bed towns along different private lines across the city is that they all look and feel pretty much the same. This is true of megalopolises the world over, but it's even truer in Tokyo, because of the vastness of the new development compared to the paucity and insignificance of what went before. There are few old buildings to give the new development a hint of character, and as all are set down on the great plain of Musashi, nothing much in the way of distinctive natural features, either. Moreover, the society's conformist tendency means that both architecturally and in terms of facilities provided—a bit of a park, a shopping mall with a sort of French name—the bed towns of Tokyo are much of a dreary muchness.

With few intrinsic qualities to help the would-be resident make up his mind, his criteria of choice are pretty objective: how much does it cost? and, how far is it from work? When the advertisements go up for new developments, those are always the factors displayed in the biggest type:

3LDK [= three rooms with living/dining-room-cum-kitchen] from ¥19,950,000 [= about $80,000]
3-minutes' walk from the station
32 minutes from Ikebukuro

The new Tokyo family, in fact, does not really live in a *place* at all: it lives a given distance from a place. Nor—go and see for yourself—does the place where it lives feel like a real place. Beyond the swollen, ungainly concrete boxes of the department stores by the nearest station, the features of each development are almost identical: blocks of housing with pressed metal balconies and bars over the windows, like oversized chicken coops; tracts of little pseudo-Californian detached houses, each on its own little slab of sandy land, with its white stucco walls and jolly blue roof tiles.

"People," wrote Fumihiko Maki, architect and professor at Tokyo University, "do not and cannot have a distinct image of today's megalopolis in its entirety. The image that most residents have of the city is only a diagram . . . on which [is] plotted the knowledge of the very few parts of the city with which they are familiar." Maki mentions the subway map, but perhaps the best example is the special rail map folded away inside the huge, phone-directory-like guides for house hunters published weekly. It's a beautiful thing. It's two feet wide and about eight inches high. Every national, private, and subway station in the whole megalopolis can be found there, but what really makes it special is that you can tell from a glance exactly how many minutes any given branch-line station is from any terminus. That's why they call it, using English, a "Time Map." You can instantly tell whether by moving from X to Y you will lengthen your journey to and from work or shorten it, and by how much; it enables you to figure out in a trice

56

THE VILLAGE DREAM

"West No. 2 Estate"—the section previously offered—"all sold out on the first day." Hurry! Hurry!

"East No. 1 Estate, First Block."

Echoes both of Manhattan style and old English solidity in the use of Roman letters and the choice of name and typeface for this section of the estate.

Abundantly green yet with big-city facilities. "Hai Kuwaliti" (High-quality) living space.

"April 13 (Saturday): Moderu rumu opun!" To ascertain the quality, do not hesitate to visit the model room.

Plans of the three types of apartment unit on offer. 2A (extreme left) is a "2LDK," that is, an apartment with two bedrooms and a living room with attached dining room-cum-kitchen. Six units in this format are available. 3AL (center) is a "3LDK" (three bedrooms), with eleven units available, and 4AL is a "4LDK" (four bedrooms), of which there are also eleven units.

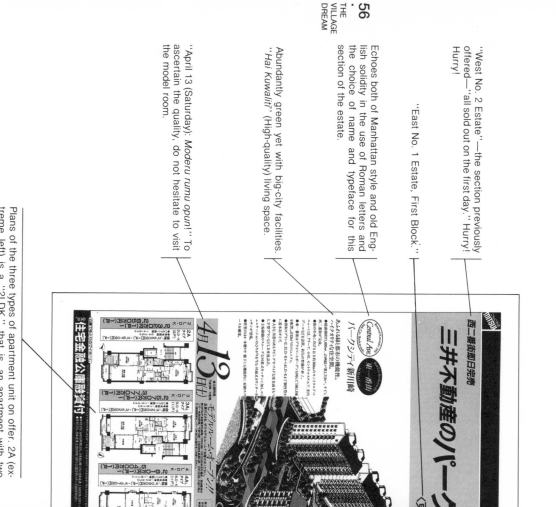

"Mitsui Real Estate's Park City Shin-Kawa-saki." Mitsui follows common practice in giving their new estate an "elegant" English name. They might equally have chosen a French one.

"*Konnichi wa, Mitsui desu*": "Hi, this is Mitsui speaking." Friendly, approachable—and one of the two biggest real estate companies in the land. (The other is Mitsubishi.)

"*Shin Hatsu Bai*"—"newly for sale"—invariable refrain to a million commercials, tagged to everything from real estate to new blends of whisky.

The crucial information, raison d'être of the whole estate: twenty-one minutes to Tokyo Station, ten minutes to Yokohama Station. Shin ("New")-Kawasaki is not a new station, but several years ago the JNR's Yokosuka Line was rerouted through it, directly linking the centers of both Tokyo and Yokohama. This forlorn and dilapidated suburb was instantly transformed into a desirable place to live. Just how desirable is made clear in the maps, which show Shin-Kawasaki's relation to the surrounding rail network (*upper*), and to the nearest station (*lower*).

Readers are quietly reminded of the Mitsui organization's venerability (it was established as a kimono store way back in the Edo period) by the inclusion of its premodern logo.

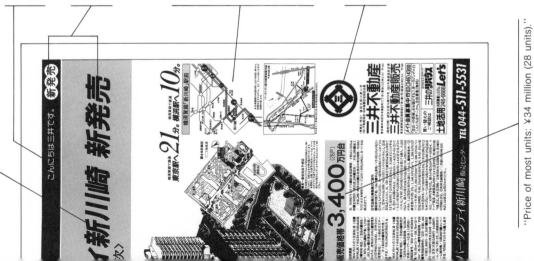

"Price of most units: ¥34 million (28 units)." Approximately $136,000.

whether the extra expense of living closer in will be adequately compensated by the shorter time you need to spend each morning wedged inside somebody's armpit . . . or vice versa. On that one map is concentrated a great deal of what the Tokyo resident bent on surviving needs to know.

Because the breadwinner of modern Tokyo is the new nomad, and like the Bedouin and the tribes that traverse the steppes of Central Asia the conditions in which he must undertake his wandering are the most important facts of his life. It was Arnold Toynbee who, in *Cities on the Move*, drew attention to this striking new fact of urban life. Our Jewish and Christian ancestors, he wrote, "were familiar with [the] nomadic way of life at second hand, but few of them had ever set eyes on a contemporary pastoral horde. . . . Our seventeenth century ancestors would have been astonished—and probably incredulous—if it had been foretold them that the mobility which was being suppressed in its traditional form was now going to shift its venue to the hitherto sedentary world."

The new nomad of Tokyo wanders in from his noplace in the wilderness, and if he barges into the nestlike centers of the old city, each with its concentrated sense of place and history, he is an utter stranger. That's part of the sadness of the contemporary city: that the sections which cradle, as the cells of a honeycomb cradle honey, the richest distillation of the city's essence, have nothing whatever to do with the lives and feelings of the mass of the city's people.

⧺

Traveling rather than settling is the central fact of the life of the new Tokyoite, and it was thus with a sure instinct that Kisho Kurokawa, one of Japan's internationally famous architects, developed his theory and practice of "capsule architecture" some fifteen years ago.

The West has mockingly dismissed Japan's miniature living spaces as "rabbit hutches," and the Japanese had a hard job putting any more pleasingly modern or sophisticated complexion on them until Kurokawa came along. As the American Mercury space program started to roll, he was quick to notice that the most glamorous American living environment of all time was also so cramped it made the Japanese tea cottage look like a villa in Pacific Palisades. It was of course the space capsule, and for Kurokawa it spelled not so much the rehabilitation of small spaces as the revolutionizing of the concept of the room.

As Kurokawa conceived it, the box that went up into space was one type of capsule; the *kago*, the palanquin in which feudal lords were lugged around the country in the old days, was another; the automobile yet another. And viewed from this perspective, the room—in particular the neat, compact, modular Japanese room—was simply a capsule that stayed in one place, a capsule for living in.

A capsule [Kurokawa wrote in his *Capsule Declaration*] is a dwelling of *Homo movens*. The rate at which city dwellers move home in the United States is around 25 per cent a year. Soon the rate in Japan will exceed 20 per cent a year. Urban size can no longer be measured in terms of night-time (residential) population. The night-time population taken together with the day-time population, or the pattern of movement of the population throughout the day, will become the index of the features of city life. People will gradually lose their desire for property such as land and big houses and will begin to value having the opportunity and the means for free movement. The capsule means emancipation of a building from land and signals the advent of an age of moving architecture.

Kurokawa's capsule was a stroke of genius. Prefabricate it in a factory like a car, and pre-fit it, like a spaceship, with a decent set of technopop gizmos—and suddenly the little ol' rabbit hutch was back in business!

In its perfected form, Kurokawa's inspiration has only been realized once: in the Nakagin Capsule Building, in the Ginza section of central Tokyo. The building's jagged profile is every bit as daring as its conception, and it looks pretty striking even now, twelve years or more after its completion. All the residential units are steel truss boxes, modified shipping containers, appropriately enough, which were fitted out in the factory with

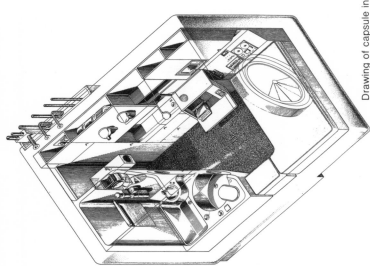

Drawing of capsule interior.

bathrooms, beds, TVs, and audio equipment and then driven to the site by truck and hooked up on to the concrete superstructure. The haphazard, unfinished look of the thing was deliberate: Kurokawa's message was that the modern building should be willing and able to change at any time. The owner might even elect to have his capsule unhooked and shipped across the seas with a bunch of other containers—though this has apparently never happened.

Kurokawa's building proved too expensive to be repeated, but his capsule inspiration led directly to one of the most extraordinary new features of the Japanese urban scene: the capsule hotel.

They're everywhere now, in every major city. Unlike Kurokawa's creation, the capsule hotel is nothing to look at, just the standard ferroconcrete pile. Inside, however, it's something else. There are no rooms; instead there are boxes, seven feet long by three feet wide by three feet high, piled two or three high and ar-

▼ Exterior of the Nakagin Capsule building.

ranged in long lines. You enter the box either through the front or the side, depending on the design; inside there is a built-in TV, radio, air conditioner, and reading light.

I've had the misfortune to spend several nights in capsule hotels; the initial feeling of coziness is rapidly replaced by a suffocating sense of confinement, made worse by the fact that the air conditioners are usually busted. And there always seems to be some drunk in the next box but one who spends the night elaborately lighting cigarette after cigarette, while one lies awake waiting for the place to go up in a puff of toxic smoke.

Unpleasant though it undoubtedly is, the capsule hotel has caught on in a big way because it fulfills a need: the need of the low-grade white-collar *sarariman* (salaried worker) and the traveling salesman with a miserable expense budget to alight in central Tokyo, snatch some sleep, and spend almost nothing—less than 4,000 yen, when the cheapest conventional hotel room would cost half that much again. It's a way of being part of the big city for the night with the smallest possible commitment of funds.

The fundamental difference between a capsule and a real dwelling is that the latter has a symbiotic relation to the land on which it stands; it has roots, if you like. The car, the spaceship, and the palanquin, because in their operational state they are always on the move, have none.

And Kurokawa's capsule building and the capsule hotel, though they are rooted in the earth, *desire* none; the illusion they exist to foster is that you can stand still in one place, yet be as free and footloose as the wind.

Arnold Toynbee wrote, "The replacement of the tiny walled city by the boundless city of the present and the future has changed the character of the crux of urban life. In a traditional city the crux was the congestion of a stationary population.... In a present-day megalopolis the crux is the congestion of the traffic now that the population has become mobile." Coming in from his dormitory no-place to the center of the city, the new nomad checks into a capsule hotel—thereby leaving no doubt as to which side of the historical equation he is on.

3

THE RIGHTEOUS AND THE DAMNED

In 1984 British journalist Polly Toynbee and her husband and daughter received a mysterious invitation to visit Japan. It came from Daisaku Ikeda, head of a Buddhist sect called Soka Gakkai. Wonderingly, they accepted. They had no idea what they had let themselves in for.

We arrived at Tokyo Airport [Toynbee wrote later in the *Guardian*], and at least ten people were there to greet us, with a huge bouquet each for my husband and for Milly, my astounded twelve-year-old daughter. A long solemn message of welcome from Mr. Ikeda was read out, and we were driven away in a vast black limousine with electric darkened windows and Mr. Ikeda's emblem emblazoned on the carpet in gold thread . . . .

Two representatives from the English branch of Mr. Ikeda's movement had accompanied us all the way from London and were scarcely to leave our side, together with a phalanx of interpreters, drivers and aides of all kinds. "Mr. Ikeda wishes you to feel entirely at home," and "Mr. Ikeda wishes you to make every use of the hotel's services and thirty-six restaurants," came the messages at regular intervals as we gazed out of our fourteenth floor window on to the hotel garden—full of waterfalls, bridges and carp, squeezed, like everything in Tokyo, between intersecting flyovers. . . .

The evening came when we were at last to meet [Mr. Ikeda]. The great black limousine pulled into the palatial head-quarters. The doorway was floodlit with camera lights, and there stood Mr. and Mrs. Ikeda, surrounded by bowing aides and followers. Dazed and dazzled by this unexpected reception committee, we were led up to him to shake the small, plump hand. There he stood, a short, round man with slicked down hair, wearing a sharp Western suit. Camera bulbs flashed, movie cameras closed in, and we were carried away with the throng, past corridors of bowing girls dressed in white to an enormous room.

Vast white armchairs were arranged in a huge square and we were ushered to a throne-like set of three chairs at the head of the room, one for each of us and one for Mr. Ikeda. He speaks no English, so behind us sat his beautiful young interpreter. . . .

We sat there awed, appalled, intimidated, while royal courtesies flowed. "I want you to feel absolutely at home this evening," said Mr. Ikeda, as we felt about as far from home as it is possible to be. "Just enjoy yourselves on this very informal occasion," he said. What would a formal meeting have been like?

The reason for the invitation and the five-star reception, they obliquely managed to gather later, was that Mr. Ikeda was hoping to tighten the public connection between himself and Polly Toynbee's famous grand-father, Arnold Toynbee, the prophet of the rise of the East. A volume of conversations between the two men had been published as a result of Ikeda's efforts years earlier, and the link did Ikeda's intellectual respectabili-ty no end of good. As a result, as Polly Toynbee wrote, "We were to see a rather different side of Japan from the view usually offered to Western visitors."

Soka Gakkai is the largest and most influential of Japan's "new religions," and Toynbee conveys the flavor of the phenomenon well: the ostentatious wealth, the pretentious public displays, the stiltedly decorous behavior, the sense of a rigid hierarchy behind it all—not to mention the unashamed and luxurious world-liness of the leader. Daisaku had "ample features," she wrote; he was "worldly . . . . earthy almost, without a whiff of even artificial spirituality. . . . I have met many powerful men—prime ministers, leaders of all kinds—but I have never in my life met anyone who exudes such an aura of absolute power as Mr. Ikeda. . . . I am not easily frightened, but something in him struck a chill down my spine." As if to prove her point about worldliness, a few weeks after her report appeared the Japanese papers went to town on the confessions of a defector from the movement who claimed she had twice been forced to have sex with the great teacher.

What does it all add up to, this religion without spirituality, this plumped-up, slicked-down Buddhism in a sharp suit?

#

Japan is the only non-Western country in history which has succeeded in exchanging poverty for riches, agriculture for industry, and a rural population for an urban one. In fact Japan's pulled the trick off not once but twice: for several years after defeat in the last war Japan was so poor that as far as the rest of the world was concerned it was back in the ranks of the "underdeveloped." And now—it is not merely "industrial," not merely "advanced"; it is in absolute terms the second greatest industrial power in the world, after the United States.

Uniquely, Japan's gone from the bottom to the top. Within a century and a bit its national experience has encompassed, materially and psychologically, that of both the world's poorest countries and the richest. And its society has felt the strains and tensions peculiar to both, too. In a way experienced by no other country, Japan's history has been telescoped. If its contemporary society has unique features, that's the main reason—not, as some Japanese like to believe, because they are a special race of people, to whom the rest of the world's rules do not apply, but because, in their fleeting dash through the twentieth century, they have managed to catch both Asian and Western ailments, and have compounded them into something quite interesting and alarming.

The problems in the Japanese papers today are rich-country problems: delinquency at school, drug addiction, rising divorce rates, violence in the streets, housewife frustration. And the nice things are rich-country things, too: sports cars, fantastic fashions, world travel, a dinky little leisure boom.

Then a bizarre phenomenon like Soka Gakkai leaps out and punches you on the snout and you ask yourself—where the hell did *that* come from?

‡

Japan's international prominence is nothing new: as long ago as 1919 Japan was considered powerful enough to be accorded big-power status at the Treaty of Versailles. Yet the draining of the rural population into the great cities, the process which occurred in Western Europe in the second half of the nineteenth century, did not get seriously under way here until after the Second World War.

In 1940, 44 percent of the working population was in farming, fisheries, and mining—mostly farming. By 1960 this had dropped to 32.7 percent, and at present it stands at about 10 percent. Though higher than the proportion in farming in the most industrialized countries of Western Europe—the figure in Great Britain, for example, is only 2 percent—it is many percentage points lower than the figure for any of Asia's other industrializing nations. South Korea's farmers, for example, constitute 24 percent of the work force, Taiwan's 23 percent, and India's 32 percent.

The ratio of urban to rural workers is thus comparable to that of Western Europe; yet the speed at which this switchover of population from countryside to city was accomplished is comparable to the rate at which it is happening in other parts of Asia now—in other words, much, much faster than anything that was ever experienced in Europe. It would not perhaps be unreasonable to expect cities of Japan to betray some of the signs of strain that so notoriously afflict the cities of its poorer Asian neighbors.

Shanty towns, for example: in India or the Philippines a high birthrate and the adoption of more efficient, less labor-intensive farming methods mean that more and more country children grow up to find there is no work for them on the land. They drain toward Calcutta or Manila where there is no room for them and no welcome, and in the end they join one of the shanty-town communities that are helping to swell the populations of those cities by 6 or 7 percent every year.

The same thing has been happening in Japan over the past forty years: a comparable proportion of the rural population, finding farming to be less and less economic, has drifted toward the big cities. The difference: in Japan there were always jobs available, and most of the immigrants were able to find themselves at least a rudimentary sort of apartment. So although Japan's cities have slum sections, shanty-town-like areas are rare.

And yet the social problems of which the shanty town is such a vivid symbol are to a great extent shared by the migrants of Japan: the loss of the long-established, dependable, slow-changing village order; confusion over identity and morality arising from that; a sense of inferiority vis-à-vis the city and the people who seem so effortlessly to belong to it.

In Southeast Asia the uprooted countryman gravitates to the shanty town where, whatever the hardship and squalor, he at least has the fellowship of people very similarly placed. His counterparts in Japan, however, do not have that consolation; they are dispersed through the bewildering void of the city like water poured into water, passing in one drastic step from a small community where everybody knows everybody, to a place with no boundaries, where everybody is a stranger.

As Tokyo has neither ghettos nor shanty towns, it is easy to forget about this sizable chunk of the population. Especially for the *gaijin*, the foreigner, so painfully and continuously aware himself of being an outsider, it is easy to lapse into the mistake of thinking that all the lookalike Japanese belong to the place equally.

Yet though the newcomers from the countryside were dispersed through the city, they did not dissolve into it; they did not stay invisible forever. Before long the new institutions they had created—the new religions—broke out on the city's face like monstrous carbuncles. Soka Gakkai was just the biggest.

Soka Gakkai is not in fact the best for our purposes. The most lurid, the most ripely carbuncular—at least in terms of its architecture—is a sect called Reiyukai, with its inner-city headquarters and symbol, the building called Shakaden ("Buddha Hall").

You could walk past Shakaden day after day—it's near one of the capital's most popular tourist routes, the one which leads from the Hotel Okura and the U.S. Embassy to Tokyo Tower and Sojoji Temple—and never suspect you were missing anything special. Then one day, glancing up at the diminutive wooden buildings of the local Shinto shrine on the hill there, you might notice above them a steeply pitched segment of huge black roof with an odd double-ring arrangement balanced on

Shakaden, temple of the Reiyukai sect.

top, and feel curious enough to take the next narrow turning on the right and see what it's about.

And there, wedged into the little street, is this monstrous *thing*. . . . If the architectural value of a building has anything to do with the fertility with which it pollinates images in the observer's mind, Shakaden is a work of genius. What *is* it? A dinosaur in a tight spot? A helmeted samurai warrior with his tongue hanging out? The mating of a Buddhist temple and a flying saucer? Or is it, as the Reiyukai people themselves suggest,

"Two hands placed together in an attitude of prayer"? Its monstrous red Brazilian granite and stainless steel bulk looms over the small plaza and the humble miscellaneous jumble squeezed in around the fringes, awesomely self-assertive but also oddly pathetic, like a great bully with a harelip. What exactly is it trying to say?

On balance, the temple/flying saucer image may be the most telling. Certainly it sits there like something that has just landed, and may any minute blast off again, and climbing the steep steps into the cavernous opening feels much like the climax of a Steven Spielberg film. Yet a Buddhist temple is what, functionally, it is, and the temple of what is, in doctrinal terms, quite a mainstream sect.

Like Soka Gakkai and another of the most successful of the new religions, Rissho Kosei Kai, Reiyukai's teaching derives from a fourteenth-century figure named Nichiren. A uniquely intolerant and fanatical Buddhist priest in a country where the more customary attitude to religion is one of benign pluralism, Nichiren was extraordinarily successful in recruiting followers from among the common people. The truculence of his language and behavior were captivating to the oppressed; his simple, formulaic approach to salvation, which depended on regularly and mechanically chanting the Lotus Sutra, could be understood by everybody. While other sects declined to the status of glorified undertakers' businesses, the Nichiren sect retained its voltage down the centuries.

And the same mixture of zeal and simplicity proved irresistible earlier this century when the uprooted farmers who had come pouring into the cities began yearning for social forms to substitute for the tight and all-embracing village structures they had left behind. As a symbol, the angry, pious outsider Nichiren was magnetically attractive. Yet the sect through which his teaching had long been channeled, with its quaint old temples and professional priests, was irrelevant to the new age.

All the founders of Japan's major new religions, both the charismatics and the solid, opportunistic business types who supported them, were of migrant origin, either born in the country and coming to the capital as young adults, or born of poor country families that had themselves moved to the city in the recent past. And the deep meaning of the organizations they founded was not obscurely mystical or spiritual. Incense smoke may play about the temples they built, and millions of people undoubtedly draw consolation from the prayers and consultations which take place in them. But at the level of unconscious purpose there was indeed not a trace of "even artificial spirituality" about them.

The new religions are best understood as the collective ego of the uprooted. Down the ages the rice farmer was always beset by poverty, but in compensation he was allowed virtue; indeed, with his diligence and productivity he was the very type of Japanese virtue, and during the long Tokugawa period, from the early 1600s until 1868, this fact was acknowledged by according him second place in the social hierarchy, below only the samurai.

The U.S. Occupation reforms after the last war took away the farmers' poverty, but in the years of economic growth that followed, his immemorial dignity was ripped away from him, too; suddenly, it seemed, a different sort of person had become the salt of the earth, source of the nation's wealth: the merchant, formerly the lowest of the low, a short way above the untouchables.

The new religions, it seems to me, are an instrument of vengeance for the farmers against that state of affairs. That's why their piety, perfunctory as it is, stresses veneration of the ancestors: honor the noble line! That's why their leaders wear business suits, drive around in limousines, and grow fat, for their aim is to beat the merchants at their own status game, the quintessential expression of which is the business corporation. That's why their symbolic buildings squat in central Tokyo with the insolent assertion of giant reptiles. . . .

One of the things that makes Tokyo a fascinating city to watch is that it allows these peculiar dinosaurs to wade in and plonk themselves down. The traditional city, as we have seen, was made of wood. Its buildings were small in scale and inarticulate. It's one of the peculiarities of Japanese civilization that it never developed a monumental architecture, nor any of the urban features—broad streets, crescents, plazas—in which monumental buildings are seen to advantage. Not even the villas of the rich were designed to be looked at except close up. They hid behind thick mud walls.

Modern architecture arrived in force only after the war. Hard, superexpressive, and apparently permanent, it landed with a squelching impact. There was no way for it to fit in, to enter into some kind of a relationship with the buildings that were there already, no criteria by which it could be judged harmonious or otherwise. As one of the badges of power in Japan's new postwar world, a large and flashy building was the thing to have. When the money and the ambition were there, the buildings got built, and except for the imposition of some highly fixable volume restrictions, there was nothing anyone could do to stop them.

Modern Tokyo's skyline, therefore, is not beautiful, but it is a pretty faithful reflection of the realities of power. It's dynamic, too; it never stops changing. And in its endless, anarchic shifting and shaking down, it sometimes captures some aspect of the process of change with a fidelity hard to match with mere words.

Next to the Reiyukai's extraterrestrial temple, for example (almost underneath it, in fact), is the small Shinto shrine mentioned earlier. It's called Hachimangu because its tutelary deity is the Shinto god Hachiman—the god of war, as it happens (*gu* means "shrine"). Like similarly humble little shrines all over the country, it is the spiritual center of the local community. From here the *o-mikoshi*, the portable shrine, sets out on the shoulders of the young artisans and shopkeepers on festival day; here parishioners come when they feel in need of a little divine assistance, to assure a successful birth or heal a family quarrel, pulling on the rope above the offering box to rattle the rusty-sounding bell before praying.

But this community's in trouble: its scale is too small for this quarter of the twentieth century, its economic activity too petty, its buildings too frail—and the land it sits on, not a mile from the city center, way too valuable. Bit by bit the land is being bought up; one by one the families are moving away to suburbia, to try and find a new identity for themselves there. The shrine's in trouble, too, looking a little dilapidated now. The priestess is only a part-timer, and no one's got a good word to say for her.

While the poor whose ancestors were born in the heart of the city are dispossessed, the energetic and vengeful boys from the country pour in. Nothing captures that seesaw swing of the society better than the tatty little shrine, with the enigmatic bulk of the Shakaden looming up behind it.

Yet Tokyo's inner city has produced its own whiz kids, too. Perhaps the most remarkable and significant of them is Taikichiro Mori, the property developer.

#

Taikichiro Mori is a patriarch of enormous wealth and power who has put himself practically beyond the reach of the media. My own meeting with him took months to set up, and was perhaps only agreed to because I was a foreigner who had previously written several articles (none of them too friendly) about his firm's effect on Tokyo. The build-up to the meeting had the mood of a Triad sequence in a Chinese gangster movie.

The conference room on the fourteenth and top floor of the sleek new office building, one of Mori's own, was dominated by a huge, highly polished oval table. Aides escorted us to our appointed places. Three of Mori's immaculate amanuenses filed in and sat in a line against the back wall, and took out pens and notebooks. Another sat opposite us at the big table. Weighty pleasantries were lobbed across the room. Green tea was served, like a sacrament.

Our eyes kept returning to the one empty chair, a soft orange swiveler. Mori's.

The door opened and all rose. The man who has done more than any other individual to change the face of the world's largest city padded in, wearing a charcoal gray kimono, black *haori* divided trousers, and black split-toed socks. He looked as frail and sensitive as a haiku poet.

The frailty is no affectation, for Taikichiro Mori has

turned eighty and suffers from angina. His intelligence and clarity of mind are undimmed, however. In the course of an hour and a bit's discussion the gently irresistible and thoroughly Japanese philosophy which has guided his rise from local rice-merchant's boy to Japan's third biggest landowner, bettered only by Mitsubishi and Mitsui, came through vividly.

Mori is not only one of the biggest but also far and away the most visible property developer in Tokyo. Anybody who learns to read a few Chinese characters soon starts to spot his firm's logo, plastered high up on office buildings across a broad section of the inner city. All his office buildings—though not his apartment houses, nor the buildings developed jointly with other concerns—bear the words "Mori Biru" (i.e., "Mori Building") and a number, with Mori Biru 43 the latest in the series. Looking up from almost any street in Toranomon, the Mori heartland, it is hard to avoid spotting at least two or three.

To the Western mind there's something downright sinister and Kafkaesque about all this, especially when, as has happened recently, Mori teams up with the Japanese freemasons to create so-called Masonic Mori Buildings.

Mori's own explanation is straightforward and homely, and knocks something of a hole in one's journalistic resolve to suspect the worst.

"I look on my buildings as if they were my children," Mori told me, "and like children I give them names. 'Mori' is the family name, then I give them numbers, just as Japanese forenames—Ichiro, Jiro, Saburo, and so on—often contain numbers, to indicate the child's place in the sequence. That's the reason."

‡

Taikichiro Mori's achievement and significance can only be understood against the background of how Tokyo has developed during the past century.

Since its foundation four centuries ago, Tokyo has divided naturally into two distinct parts: the "Yamanote," or "high city" as Edward G. Seidensticker renders it, the hilly sections starting slightly inland of

Tokyo Bay; and the *shitamachi*, the "low city," the low-lying areas, some of them actually reclaimed from the sea, between the hills and the bay. To call them the west end and the east end gives a pretty clear idea of the way they divided up, both geographically and in terms of class (though there were anomalies which I will come to shortly).

Yamanote was the salubrious zone, the upland slopes which stayed relatively cool and pest-free even in summer. Here the shogun's retainers built their spreading villas, behind those thick mud walls. Later, when the shogun made it compulsory for the ruling lords in the provinces to spend one year in two in the capital, and to billet their families there permanently, it was in these same hilly regions that they built their new homes.

Some fine aristocratic villas sprang up along the bay, too, but the population of the flat areas was overwhelmingly proletarian. It was here that the artisans and laborers and merchants who served and catered to the aristocracy settled and put down roots. The flatlands were hot, pestiferous, liable to flood and fire, and the worst hit in every earthquake. But in one respect the "east end" tag does not quite fit, for it was the shitamachi which was the city's cultural heart, too. As the home of the economically rising but still socially stigmatized class of merchants, the shitamachi was the heart of the culture which their wealth and fancy brought into being. Most of the artistry with which the rest of the world identified Japan in the nineteenth century was the product of the shitamachi: the Kabuki theater, the ukiyoe print, and much else. Yoshiwara, the "nightless city," the pleasure quarter near Asakusa in the northeast, was the center of that world.

As Seidensticker recounts in his book about Tokyo, *Low City, High City*, the shitamachi and the culture identified with it suffered a series of crushing setbacks during the first half-century of modernization: earthquakes, floods, fires, and finally and most disastrously, the great fire that followed the earthquake of 1923. Yet, though the cultural traditions began crumbling away under this multiple impact—or, in some cases, upped stakes with the newly emancipated merchants and moved west—

the dense population, squashed, most of them, into microscopic plots of land, stayed put.

The situation in Yamanote was very different. With the collapse of the shogunate, the shogun's retainers and dependent lords no longer had any business in the capital and returned to their home provinces. With their departure, many acres of the city's choicest land fell vacant. This was the land on which the modern, Westernized city grew. Foreign legations snapped up many of the best bits. Close to the palace and between the inner and outer moats, the institutions of the new state came into being: barracks, courts, police headquarters. Right opposite the palace reared the columns and architraves and mansard roofs of the nation's first real hotel, the Imperial.

The old city had many temples, too: persecuted by new laws designed to create a Shinto-based state, many Buddhist sects were forced to relinquish spacious properties in the city. In their place rose schools and universities, derived, like everything else that was new and flourishing, from Western models.

Through all this tumultuous activity, the *minkan* or "popular" sections of the city remained almost unchanged. There were disastrous fires, but fire was one of the hazards of city life to which shitamachi people had long become inured. *Edo no hana* they called them, "Edo's flowers," as if the flames were no more than decorations for their coats. After the fires they rebuilt, on the same plots and in the same flammable way. Unlike the shogun's samurai, *they* had no reason to move, no place else to go, and no room to expand, either. Even after the terrible destruction of the last months of the war, reconstruction went ahead much as it always had. In the quieter areas, in the back streets, very little has changed for half a century; a quarter-inch of stucco and the odd half-hearted furbelow is all there is to distinguish the new from the very old indeed.

All this is true across a wide swath of the city's eastern flatlands. But in one pivotal minkan section called Toranomon—"Tiger's Gate"—the last twenty years have seen a dramatic change.

Toranomon is crucial because it's the minkan section

closest to Kasumigaseki, just south of the Imperial Palace, these days an area of broad avenues and big buildings and the location of many government ministries. It's Tokyo's answer to Whitehall or the Place de la Concorde. It's also the site of the 482-foot-high Kasumigaseki Building, the nation's first skyscraper, erected in 1968.

Sixty years ago, after the earthquake, the first solid government buildings were going up here. And just one traffic crossing away was Toranomon—and beyond that the scruffy heartland of the unreconstructed working class! Haunt of carpenters, mechanics, jobbing printers, rice dealers, buckwheat-noodle makers, clacking around on clogs from the tofu shop to the public bath as if Commodore Perry's black ships had never put out!

It would obviously never do. Yet it *might* have done, it might have gone on indefinitely, had Toranomon not also been the home of Taikichiro Mori, the rice dealer's son.

Mori was born and raised here. His ancestors had lived in the city for 150 years. His father combined rice dealing with landlordship, but the properties he owned nearby were typical wooden post-and-beam structures, two stories high at the most. They inhabited a different world from the new stone, brick, and concrete behemoths just half a mile to the north.

⌗

Tokyo's flatlands had been incinerated three times during the life of Mori's grandfather and the same thing happened again, on an even worse scale than before, after the disastrous earthquake of September 1, 1923. The Mori's home was one of the hundreds of thousands that burned down.

Mori was only nineteen at the time, but he was quick to see the way things were tending. "After the Great Earthquake many modern concrete buildings were put up, some with the help of government grants," he said. "I gave voice to the new thinking and urged my father to rebuild in concrete, but I was told it was too early for that. So I helped him rebuild in wood."

The wisdom of young Mori's view was proved by the

speed with which yet another rebuilding became necessary, for as a result of the incendiary bombing in 1945, huge areas of Tokyo were razed once again. This time Mori, by now Professor of Commerce at a university in Yokohama, was old and important enough to impose his ideas.

"Above all I was thinking about how to prevent Tokyo burning again. . . . After the war damage it became apparent that the normal small wooden dwellings were no longer any good, and that they must be replaced with nonflammable ones. This necessity became even more obvious after our defeat by the nations of the West. . . . The ordinary old Japan could not survive, it would be defeated by the advanced nations, so we had to struggle to achieve rapid Westernization.

"After the fire I started sorting through the rubble, keeping the patches of land on which I thought I could someday build offices and selling others I didn't think suitable. . . . While the people all around were throwing up their rabbit-hutch houses, we didn't build. We kept our plots open. It wasn't until 1955, ten years later, that we constructed our first building, Mori Biru 1."

Erected just south of the outer moat (filled in) of the Imperial Palace, Mori's first concrete baby had a lobby that was little better than a cubby hole. It was a full ten stories in height, however, and it made a big impact. "We were surprised by the response," Mori says. "I realized then that my way of thinking could be successful from the business point of view. That's how we got started."

Thus began the conversion of Toranomon into a section full of large, bland office buildings scarcely distinguishable from those of any other city in the world. It was the beginning of Toranomon's evacuation, its metamorphosis into a sort of glassy ghost town. Tokyo's proletarian communities had endured for hundreds of years, surviving fires, floods, earthquakes, typhoons . . . yet confronted with Taikichiro Mori they appeared helpless to resist. Meekly they packed up their things and stole away.

How did he manage it? That's the question that keeps demanding an answer. Besides being the safest possible investment, property has an almost sacred significance for the Japanese. Possession of it binds them in two ways, in time and space: in time, to the ancestors from whom it is inherited and to whom they owe their own existence; in space, to the community into which they are born, the community which provides them with most of their most vital relationships. For the old Tokyo townsman, his land was quite literally the ground of his being. He was lost without it.

So strong and difficult to violate are these ties that Tokyo's authorities have had to resort to desperate measures to modernize the city. Roads were widened with great difficulty, and the only way they could put in expressways was to run them in over the tops of existing roads on concrete stilts, thereby creating some of the most infernally noisy and polluted urban canyons anywhere on earth. When a major overspill area was deemed necessary to ease congestion at the center, they were obliged to fill in a water purification plant—at Shinjuku—and locate their skyscrapers there.

Only Mori seems to possess some sort of magic immunity; he alone seems able to do with the city's land pretty well what he pleases. How does he manage it?

One reason is that success of the sort Mori has achieved breeds more and more success, thanks to the iron laws of taxation. The *koteishisan*, "fixed property tax," which all Japanese homeowners pay annually on their property, is reassessed every three years, and as office buildings, Mori's and others', multiply in the Toranomon area, pushing the price of property higher and higher, the tax burden on the residents becomes more and more intolerable. And when they die, their children are stuck with an inheritance tax bill, payable in cash, which in many cases can only be settled by selling the family land. Thus pressured, many residents are in a mood to listen to what Mori has to say.

This is only part of the explanation, however, and it begs the question of why Mori should have been able to get the ball rolling so well twenty and more years ago; why it should have been he, rather than another entrepreneur.

It is significant that most of Mori's properties are in

Taikichiro Mori with some of his aides.

Photomontage showing how Mori's new Ark Hills development will look when completed.

Toranomon, where he was born, Mori is a local boy, and heir to all those ties of obligation and dependency which bind Japanese communities. An outside developer would have less hope of wresting land away from the people here. Mori himself does not wrest it; he reasons it away. He speaks with the authority of the irresistible future, warning the people, as he told me, that "The ordinary old Japan could not survive, it would be defeated by the advanced nations." He presents these communities with the imperatives of history, but in words and terms they can understand. He does not callously kick anybody out. It's all give and take, the carefully measured doses of *giri*, of obligations inflicted and received, which characterize all dealings in Japanese society.

"The secret," one of Mori's lieutenants explains, "is to establish close relations with the local people. We go on holiday with them, for example. We take part in festivals—even helping to carry the portable shrine."

Mori is prepared to bide his time. Twenty-five small buildings used to stand on the 174,380-square-foot site now occupied by Mori Biru 40, each with a different owner, and Mori had to secure the cooperation of each in turn before he could go forward. The process took eight years.

Sometimes it is merely a matter of waiting under the tree for the ripe fruit to drop off. Tokyo's wooden houses age rapidly, particularly those knocked together in the grim days after the war. As they become dilapidated, so the pressure to comply with Mori's wishes grows stronger—for the alternative is an expensive (and, in the circumstances, whimsical) rebuilding. "We've had failures, sites we've had to give up on," Mori's man confesses, "but not many."

Mori is not, after all, asking the existing owners to sell outright; he is not necessarily asking them even to vacate their land altogether. Flexibility is another characteristic of Mori's operation, and arrangements vary. In the case of, say, a flourishing restaurant, the owner, in return for relinquishing his plot, may get space in the new building equivalent to its agreed worth. This enables him to open a restaurant on the ground floor of the new building and then, after selling off the rest of his share in it, buy or rent a house in commuter-land, a few stops down the subway track.

By this means, without compulsory purchase orders, threats, or overt bad feeling of any kind, residential land is quietly converted to commercial use, and the inner-city townsman transformed into a commuter.

However humane the methods, the net result of Mori's work is the decimation of inner-city communities, a deterioration in the quality of life of those that remain, and a steep drop in tax revenue for the local authority. But at last, in the latest and grandest project of his career, a compromise has been reached between Mori, the residents in the way of his development, and local government, which may mark a historic turning point for Tokyo's inner city.

Ark Hills is the largest single development Tokyo has seen since the filling in of Shinjuku's reservoir fifteen years ago. The site is three and a half million square feet in area, spread across two inner-city boroughs. In the process of attempting to buy up the land, Mori encountered such determined resistance from the residents that with all his techniques of persuasion he was unable to budge them.

Minato Ward, the local municipal authority involved, waded in and worked out an agreement whereby the development would incorporate housing for the dispossessed locals as well as a hotel, swimming pool, concert hall, public space, and the inevitable office block. In fact, in response to the increasing popularity of inner-city apartments among Tokyo's young professionals, the housing in the scheme will have much greater capacity than that which has been demolished to make way for it.

Thus for the first time in Mori's vertiginously successful career, his creation of office space will not have resulted in a widening of the hole in central Tokyo's doughnut. At fifty stories and 500 feet the office block will be his highest by far, so high that standing volume restrictions had to be bent backwards to let it through. This looks suspiciously like the local authority's reward to Mori for his cooperation in the matter of the intransigent residents—though the Minato Ward Office (temporarily housed in yet another Mori Biru) strongly denies it.

⊞

Tokyo's most potent evangelist of the concrete future is himself an old-fashioned, scholarly man, a child of the Meiji period, who, until his heart attack four or five years ago, lived in a traditional wooden house in a hilly section of the inner city. For the sake of his own health he has swapped that now for one of his own concrete apartments. "The old house was drafty, the wind howled through, so it was cold in winter and bad for my heart," he says.

The dwelling style of the future was not immediately to the liking of this man who has imposed it on so many others, though he puts a brave face on it now. "You get used to it, you know. . . . The old house had a garden where I could do exercises and what-not in the morning—now I can't do that so I had a hemmed-in feeling at first, I couldn't relax. But now I'm so used to it I wonder how I was able to put up with such a chilly, inconvenient place before."

As if to compensate for the loss of a Japanese environment, Mori has reverted to traditional kimono since his illness. "I haven't worn Western clothes even once since then," he says. "I haven't become modernized; on the contrary I've gone right back to my roots!"

Living with his wife in semiretirement now (his son has taken over running the firm), Mori spends much of his time listening to music and reading. He reads a lot about religion, an interest he has had all his life. As a young man he was attracted to Christianity, and at the age of sixteen he had himself baptized. "After I started studying philosophy, however," he told me, "I could no longer believe in God, and graduated from Christianity"—and sixty-four years later he bought up and demolished the church where he had been baptized. These days the books he chooses to immerse himself in tend rather to deal with the Japanese religious ideas that have permeated his life and work.

"According to my way of thinking," he said, "work, the enterprise, is a form of service, a calling, bestowed on the people living in the world by God. Merely to amass money—that's not the motive; it's a matter of doing something useful to the whole society, and in order for one to be able to do this one has to make efforts to improve oneself. [The company] is a group which starts from the self-improvement of its members. That's the idea. All improve themselves in harmony. And having polished oneself like this, if you want to know what one does next, it's the calling I was talking about. In my case, building up the city. . . . To bring together people who share the same calling and do together the things necessary to achieving our shared purpose, to build up the society and the country and continue improving ourselves in the appropriate manner. . . . That's the way I want Mori Biru to be."

The leader of Soka Gakkai was described by Polly Toynbee earlier as lacking so much as "a whiff of even artificial spirituality." Odd though it may seem, Mori's interpretation of his own career and his firm's endeavor has about it a great deal more than just a whiff of spirituality, whether judged real or otherwise. According to his interpretation, the work of property development may be quite as legitimate a form of spiritual training as the Zen monk's regime of chanting and meditation.

It seems an outrageous imposture; scarcely less outrageous in its way than the worldly wise persona of the supposedly religious Daisaku Ikeda. Yet among Japanese, neither phenomenon raises an eyebrow.

Both derive from the vestigial yet still potent way the spirit of Buddhism survives in Japan's contemporary society. Much of the formal, professional structure of that religion has long since forfeited the people's respect, as plump, worldly, *namagusai* ("stinking of raw fish") youths succeeded to the priesthoods of the temples of their plump, worldly, *namagusai* fathers. Yet one of the fundamental ideas of Buddhism is still enormously attractive.

This is the ideal of egoless endeavor, the ideal of becoming one with one's work team or with the task at hand. It's an ideal that's active and influential throughout Japanese society. It's something temptingly easy for the outsider to mock as a species of simple brainwashing; yet the fact that it generates a powerful feeling of solidarity and a deep sense of satisfaction is indisputable. It's the source of much of Japan's legendary efficiency; one can read its effect equally in the statistics for the productivity of the automobile industry, and in the deftness and lightning speed of the traditional artisan.

Yet there's something wrong with this egolessness as an ideal. At its height, Japan's version of Mahayana Buddhism had as clear a moral stance as any of the great religions. With its decline, its moral content has been forgotten, or cut away as so much unneeded clutter. What remains of it in the secular society is a spiritual system lacking a moral rudder.

For the subsummation of the individual, which is what, essentially, is involved, is something that can occur in almost any organization: a car manufacturer, an army, a fake church, the firm of a properly developer.... Right after the war the Occupation authorities granted the Japanese complete religious freedom. A religious sect called Kodoji-kyo was shortly thereafter established by a clever man who had spotted a loophole in the new law that he could exploit, much like the loopholes in American law that are exploited to this day. By setting up as a church, he reasoned, any business organization could avoid payment of income tax. The owner of a restaurant, for example, could say that its purpose was to propagate the teaching that "life is religion." His customers would be devotees, and the satisfaction of hunger would be salvation. The idea proved so popular that for the next couple of years he licensed a whole variety of different businesses as churches: art shops, beauty salons, brothels.

Well, the same thing's happening today—only there are no licenses involved, and the object is no longer the evasion of income tax. Instead it is the harnessing of the total energy of the participants to the larger purposes of the organization.

If it seems dangerous, it's principally because it was exactly this combination of egolessness and moral rudderlessness, this willingness to sink oneself entirely in a common cause for which one is not required to take any intellectual responsibility, which gave Japanese militarism such an easy ride before the war. Ikeda and Mori, symbols respectively of the uprooted farmer and the inner-city merchant, reveal two different facets of the same phenomenon. It's ominous.

In Mori's case, his serene and unfeigned confidence suggests another reason for his great success. *Reject us*, he implies, *and you will be not only weak and solitary but in a sense impious, too. Come into this scheme with us, join our fellowship, and besides enriching you it will purify you.* It's an outrageous proposal: there cannot be another country in the world where it would not be laughed to scorn. But Mori says it with such egoless confidence, such perfected impersonality, that it is almost irresistible. And one by one the residents of the inner city fall into line.

Because, after all, look at the pathetic fate of those who have resisted to the bitter end! Does the city have any more vivid metaphor for the torments of hell than what they suffer?

Mr. and Mrs. Yoshitaro Muramatsu have lived in their two-story wooden house in a formerly plebeian section of town, now called Minami-Aoyama 5-chome, ever since their marriage in 1941. Yoshitaro in fact moved here with his parents six years before that, in 1935, from the house in nearby Roppongi where he was born. His wife, to whom he had been introduced at a formal matchmaking ceremony, came from Setagaya, a few miles to the southwest. Yoshitaro started a tire business in the front of the house when he came back from Shanghai at the end of the war. Their whole life was rooted in the neighborhood. All their friends were here.

But Minami-Aoyama came up in the world. During the '60s it found itself trapped between three of the most fashionable new sections of the city's west side, Aoyama, Hiroo, and Roppongi. An expressway and an almost skyscraping office block went up just down the road. Then a firm of developers proposed building a block of flats, on the very spot where the Muramatsus lived. As commuting distances lengthened from the merely painful to the ridiculous, more and more professional people were taking another look at the city center

The embattled home of Yoshitaro Muramatsu in Minami-Aoyama.

as a potential habitat. The new block would cater to them.

The developer in question was not Mori, and the approach to the residents was perhaps tougher and less humane and conciliatory than Mori's would have been. Long before agreement had been reached with the residents, for example, the developer was circulating architectural sketches of the finished block with all the existing houses conveniently erased. Owners of property on the target site were offered exchange deals, whereby they would relinquish their land in return for possession of flats in the new block.

Resentful of the developer's attitude, and suspicious of the exchange idea—"these architects are awful cunning, they never tell you what's really going on," is how he puts it now—Yoshitaro decided to refuse to have anything to do with the scheme. He simply dug in his heels. When the developer's representatives came to call he just ignored them. He put a notice out at the front of the house, among the wobbly piles of old tires: "I

WILL NOT SELL THIS LAND AND HOUSE. I REFUSE EVEN TO RENT IT."

It was an impasse. The land could not be purchased compulsorily, and the developer had far too much at stake to back down. Yoshitaro took the developer to court on the grounds that the planned building was too high for the site, but he lost. Eventually the scheme simply went ahead without the Muramatsus' participation. Their house was left *in situ*; the 113,000-square-foot block, thirteen stories at its highest point, rose behind and to the right and left of it. To stay clear of their property the design was altered marginally, and now the front wall of the apartment block and the back wall of the house are separated by inches. An eight-foot-high bamboo fence stands in between. Meanwhile the sketches of the "Demeure" block appearing in advertisements in the house-hunters' guides (copy: "Expressive of status") perpetuate the fiction that all the old dwellings have been removed. A note underneath states "[This sketch] may deviate slightly from reality."

Yoshitaro, approaching eighty, is well into retirement now, and spends much of the day pottering forlornly among the old tires and the broken clocks and umbrellas in his front room. His wife's in the hospital with an ailment he blames on their present living conditions. His eyes well with tears of effort and indignation when I ask him about the apartment block. "Yes, of course it's difficult to live here with that thing next door," he says. "It's so high, it completely blocks out the sunshine on the south side. The law says we're entitled to sunshine for three-quarters of every day, but that building makes a mockery of it. And it's dangerous, too. Have you seen the tiny size of the entranceway it's got? That's the only one, for 117 flats!" He gives a crazy cackle, wags his bristly head. "What are they going to do if there's an earthquake or a fire? It's fourteen stories at the back, and there's no space to speak of either back or front. It's against the law to build that high when there's no space in front. *Mattaku mechakucha!* It's a total nonsense!"

It's a weird sight: the apartment block with its plate glass, aluminum bollards, brass carriage lamps, and facing of white ceramic tiles, with its fashion shops and design studios at street level; and the small fragment of a different world slowly crumbling to dust in front of it, with its moth-eaten walls of old brown wood, its roof of rusty iron sheets held down by tires.

Yoshitaro Muramatsu has kept his land, but he's lost his friends, his community, nearly everything that gave his possession of land meaning. And he's gained a conspicuousness which, in this culture, no one can envy him. It's the mark of the damned.

4

LIGHTS ACROSS
THE PLAIN

For a city that is routinely described as chaotic, Tokyo has a remarkably strong and simple structure. Like all the great cities that attained greatness before the age of the expressway, its focus is a well-defined center. Within Tokyo's center are to be found all the major "control centers" of the state—Diet (Parliament), Supreme Court, police headquarters, government ministries, and so on. Several of the major museums are nearby. The main railway station is here; what is traditionally the most important shopping area is close enough to be counted in.

Yet right at the heart of it all is an enormous void—the grounds of the Imperial Palace, which covers more than 130 acres. It's so vast it seems to belong to a different city, perhaps a different civilization. The home of the emperor is here, and the offices of the Imperial Household Agency, the bureau which attends to his affairs. But for the most part the grounds belong to the realm of nature. Somewhere in the middle is a rice paddy which the emperor ceremonially cultivates year after year, the numen which clings to him forty years after he denied his own divinity helping to assure a good harvest for the rest of the nation. There used to be a nine-hole golf course somewhere in there, too; on his trip to

England in 1921 the emperor played golf with the Prince of Wales and took a fancy to the game, as he did also to soft Western beds and oatmeal for breakfast. But some years ago, it is reported, he saw rare wild flowers growing on one of the greens, and commanded that the course be allowed to return to a natural state. Now it is a wilderness.

Different values prevail in this part of town, this empty vortex of the capital's whirlpool. The roads that circle it are wide. Within them, but still outside the palace walls, a desert of gravel stretches far enough to produce mirages. Busloads of countryfolk and foreigners wander across it, blinking up at the massive stone walls beyond the waters of the inner moat.

In places the palace itself is penetrable. One of these is Higashi-Gyoen, the East Gardens, which have been open to the public only in recent years. You cross the moat, collect a plastic token at the booth, enter through the massive wooden gate: more emptiness, more roaming, lonely space. The lawns are close-clipped, edged by neat, low hedges and measured out by pine trees. Do not jog, do not play music, do not smoke as you walk along: and nobody does, because nobody lingers. Foreigners and countryfolk take a dutiful turn and leave.

Higashi-Gyoen seems the more achingly empty for all its memories of plenitude. The grounds of the Imperial Palace have not been a wilderness for long. Contemporary screen paintings show that during the early Edo period, when the palace was the headquarters of the ruling shogunate, it was the most intensively developed part of the city, crowded with large buildings, bursting with activity. The area that is now the East Gardens was the center of the whole thing: here rose the five-story donjon of the castle, the nation's largest and finest. Far more than Tokyo is today, Edo was a city of water, and the donjon was the focus of a spiral of moats, winding first tightly around its foundations, then describing wider and wider loops around the palace and the residential area of dependent lords and samurai before disgorging into the Sumida River near the bay.

That was one almost mystical way the castle's centrality was emphasized, for in the Shinto scheme the

▼ The Imperial Palace: the emptiness of the city center.

logarithmic spiral is a mystical shape, the only pictorial symbol which adequately expresses the ancient Japanese (originally Chinese) yin-yang-based conception of the workings of the universe. But the sheer size of the thing in relation to the small, congested, literally lowly city it stood at the heart of must have been awe-inspiring enough. In obedience to its beaconlike beam the city fell into place around it, radiating away from it in arcs that, though unplanned, were roughly regular.

By its height and magnificence, by its centrality, by the curling embrace of its spiral of moats, the castle bound the lower orders to itself and made of the whole one city, rigidly stratified and segregated, certainly, but visually as well as politically a single organism.

And now, where there was a castle there is nothing. There is in its place an overcultivated void. The bonds have gone slack. When, after centuries of tyranny and remoteness, the inner citadel of the East Gardens was at last, in 1968, opened to the common herd . . . they didn't want to know. For centuries they had been shunned, kept at a respectful distance; now came the chance to do a little shunning of their own.

It's the tension that has gone. The palace is still in the middle of things, but for all its relevance to the city's modern life it might as well be out in the middle of nowhere.

#

As the focus of national endeavor the emperor was rejected decisively in the aftermath of defeat in 1945. With the castle, symbol of the palace's centrality, gone too, even natives of the city tend to forget what a powerful magnet the palace has been in the city's development. The fabric of the city is so modern that it is almost impossible to find a building more than sixty years old; yet the organization of all this concrete is along lines that go back centuries.

Why, the architect Kazuhiro Ishii, a native of the city, asked himself, is urban scenic beauty of the Western type so lacking in Tokyo?

I once believed lack of enthusiasm in the design of individual buildings must account for this state of affairs [he wrote in *Japan Architect* magazine]. But later I saw that, even when some carefully designed buildings did go up, the overall condition altered little. Later, when I took the time to examine them, I saw that the plan drawings for many of the apparently negligent buildings were actually meticulously worked out. Enthusiasm had gone into their designs after all.

Then I began to think that perhaps irregularly curving streets and roads produced the disorder and chaos of the cityscape. There is no reason why roads should not curve; but, in so doing they do not lead to order among buildings that are largely rectangular solids in form or horizontally oriented slabs. Angling and bending open strange gaps among buildings and reveal their end walls in less than pleasing ways. The order inherent in the buildings themselves is unrelated to the city, with results that cannot be described as urban beauty.

The city once centered on and was concentrically placed around Edo Castle ... the [donjon] of Edo Castle (today the residence of the Emperor) however, was destroyed long ago. If I may be permitted an extravagant flight of fancy, I might say that, although the streets of the city actually revolve around the castle, they seem to forget that they do because the [donjon] that ought to be their hub is missing.

Once you notice it, the extent to which Tokyo does in fact revolve around its long-vanished hub is startling. It's not only the roads; close to the center there are the two moats, the inner and the outer, the remains of the old spiral system; further away is the Yamanote loop, the railway that joins the center with the major subcenters. Underground, the Marunouchi Line subway swings in a wide loop around the palace. And fifteen miles away there is the Musashino Railway, running through groves of trees far beyond the city's traditional boundary, yet in part following a course which has the palace as its center.

The city remains rigidly oriented along traditional lines, all eyes swiveled in the traditional direction ... yet it has, in the terms of Ishii's conceit, "forgotten" that this is so. It's as if to forget one is in chains is the same as losing them, the same as becoming free. And in this forgetful condition the developers busily put up rec-

tilinear buildings in the latest styles—and later people wonder why they do not result in the city's becoming more beautiful.

One can take this too far. Imperialism is, for most Japanese who are at all thoughtful, something which is dead and buried and can never be revived. Their neglect of the East Gardens and the feudal relationship it stands for is wholehearted.

Yet Ishii's analysis is pregnant nonetheless. When a certain French fashion designer came to Tokyo for a show, he observed the way people in the street walked. "There's something not quite modern about it," he commented. "The clothes are beautiful, but the people are not really *wearing* them yet."

⊞

If the city has forgotten that it is pointing towards the Imperial Palace, which way does it *think* it is pointing? Which way would it like to be pointing?

The only true object of emulation for the thoroughly modern metropolis is New York. But the mountain would not come to Mohammed . . . so Mohammed built a very lifelike and only slightly smaller-than-life-size model of the mountain in his backyard.

The place was called Shinjuku. Now West Shinjuku, on the outside of the Yamanote loop, is the home of nearly all the nation's real skyscrapers. But that's not the limit of Shinjuku's interest. It's a section of town with acute schizophrenia: which is to say it has two halves to it, as radically different from each other as it is possible for two parts of a single city section to get. Both in their different ways throb with the sort of life that has so plainly drained away from the environs of the palace, which has, by contrast, all the gaiety and excitement of a leper colony. West Shinjuku's life, centered now on servicing the army of office workers who inhabit its skyscrapers, may seem dryly economic, not too much like life at all. East Shinjuku, however, on the inside of the Yamanote loop, is the city's most famous modern fleshpot. It groans under the weight of a million lurid signs. It stinks. It is rife with gangsters.

In between is Shinjuku Station, the busiest and mad-

Skyscrapers in West Shinjuku. The open land is owned by the Tokyo metropolitan government, which is trying to decide what to do with it.

dest in the country. To the southwest is Shinjuku Gyoen, a former imperial garden, the emperor's old outpost on the edge of town. Let's begin our Shinjuku tour there.

⌗

Although Shinjuku Gyoen is as intimately connected to Japan's immediately imperial past as the palace over to the east, it's hard, at least at cherry-blossom time, to imagine a more gaily populistic spot.

"We live in the midst of nature," advises the notice at the entrance of the Shinjuku Imperial Garden, though on my first visit I wasn't to know that as I couldn't read. This was some years back. Two girlfriends took me there and tried to teach me the Japanese syllabaries in the space of an afternoon. It was a Sunday in April, and the cherry blossoms were at their best. Shinjuku Imperial Garden is a famous spot for *hanami*, "blossom-viewing," but being just off the boat I found the people doing the viewing more interesting than the flowers. Interesting is too weak a word. I was astonished. Some eight wickets were open at the entrance but still we had to line up to get in. Inside you couldn't see the ground for the people. In little groups on straw mats and bits of cardboard they were strewn across all 144 acres, and all were deeply involved in their time-honored cherry-blossom-viewing rituals: drinking, dancing, singing, cavorting uproariously, relishing the flavor saké acquires when the blossoms come swirling down.

"We live in the midst of nature"—perhaps, but until the end of the last war this fine bit of organized nature, with its lakes and walks and prospects, was nothing but a rumor to the common people of Shinjuku. This was imperial property, and its blossoms were for the delectation of the nobility. Then in 1945 the emperor was coaxed down from heaven, the chains fell from the gates, and the masses swarmed in.

They're still doing it, and not only here. All over Shinjuku they swarm and swarm.

A mile to the northwest, as the light of a summer day fades, the offices in the forest of big new buildings disgorge their workers into the street, and almost in a single body they move east toward the station.

This is the biggest assembly of skyscrapers in the Far East, but as recently as 1970 nothing stood here at all. Five years before that, as the reservoir of the Shinjuku Water Purification Plant, the whole place was awash with water.

By the mid-'60s, Tokyo's authorities had realized that the city's historical center and the Marunouchi business zone next to it were rapidly becoming gummed up by the thousands of extra cars and commuters created by the nation's new prosperity. "[Tokyo has become] so vast and overpopulated," suggested an official pamphlet published in 1968, "that the normal functions of the city have been hampered and life activities of the people have been disorganized to the point that energy is dissipated fruitlessly. . . .

"Therefore it has become imperative to decentralize some of the functions of the city center to the perimeter districts."

Shinjuku was the obvious first choice. Directly opposite Tokyo Station on the far side of the Yamanote loop, it was the point where that line and the east-west Chuo Line crossed, and as such it had become a major transportation center. Like practically all such centers in Japan, it had subsequently enjoyed an enormous boom in growth. And unlike any of its rivals it had buildable land—1.8 million square feet of it, once the purification plant had been shifted.

Shinjuku's history is short: as late as the turn of the present century it was no more than a fork in the road, surrounded by paddies. Now was to begin its amazing and meteoric challenge to the ancient power of the east side.

The first high-rise to go up, the Keio Plaza Hotel, was completed in 1971 on the site closest to the station. The rest followed one after another, and now there are more than a dozen. The latest to join the club are two huge hotels with curving walls, the Washington at the area's southern periphery and the new Hilton at the northern.

West Shinjuku's skyscraper park is an odd place. It's very eagerly modern—the buildings have the sort of high finish that makes many skyscrapers in other countries look shabby, and as the embodiment of the city's

Manhattan fantasies, they've done service as the backdrop to a million TV commercials and detective dramas. But of course it's not like Manhattan at all; it's just like Japan, only fifty stories high. That most venerable Japanese magic trick, in frequent use since at least the eighth century, by which they solemnly and meticulously copy some product of another culture and wind up with something unmistakably Japanese, is at work again.

Here in West Shinjuku, just as in the traditional section of Aoyama that Takamitsu Azuma walked through in chapter 2, it is not the street but the plot of land that is the dominant element in the plan. Streets there are, of course, cutting the area into a grid, but unlike Manhattan they are merely ways of getting from A to B. There are no street lines to tie the front walls of the buildings together and thereby create some impression of order. Instead, in pure local style, the skyscrapers plant themselves wherever on their plot they fancy.

When there were still only a few of them the effect, with all that windy space in between, was quite dramatic, like the stage set for some vast avant-garde production of Greek tragedy, or a new achievement in modern sculpture. Now there are so many, however, that they've practically congealed into a lump and the area looks like Tokyo all over again, only more so. If nature were to take its course, those portions of the plots presently wasted on gardens with benches, expensive restaurants, and pretentious sunken arcades would bit-by-bit be sold off to the highest bidders and new fifty-story buildings would rise, only inches from the original ones. This would not only be profitable, it would be pure Tokyo. The regulations, unfortunately, forbid it.

But there are still several complete plots left undeveloped. This seems incredible. The land in this area is not up for sale so it's hard to price it, but it can't be cheap. Across the tracks, some plots in Shinjuku are said to be worth no less than $5,350 per square foot. Yet here, practically hailing distance away, there are three 160,000-square-foot cinder patches without so much as a Mori Biru on them. What's going on?

The answer is that the land belongs to the Tokyo

metropolitan government, and they're having a terrible time trying to decide what to do with it. Twelve years have gone by and they're still no closer to a solution.

The value of the land, both financially and in terms of its location, is exactly the problem. As an expert in the city's affairs put it, the land is the city's *tora-no-ko*, its "baby tiger," its precious treasure, and the city bosses are paralyzed with indecision over how it should be used.

The present governor, Shun'ichi Suzuki, a conservative with a good track record in the matter of cutting city-hall expenses, has a grand vision. He wants to see the city government, presently divided between three large and more than twenty smaller buildings near the Imperial Palace, relocate to a fine new skyscraper here. But that's not all: Tokyo, he says, one of the greatest cities in the world, has no city hall, no place for the citizens to gather to listen to music or hold conferences. Let us build one here, he says. Something like Toronto's would do very nicely.

It's the sort of project for which the area would seem to be well suited. It would bring in people in the evenings—at present the place is desolate after office hours—and it would help to make some larger social sense of it, to make it feel real. The idea, however, has divided the city profoundly. Representatives from western sections are all for it; those from the east, from the traditional center, have dug in their heels and will resist it to the bitter end.

The center of Tokyo's population has been moving west rapidly ever since the east side was razed by 1923's earthquake. With suburbs ballooning out into the plain of Musashi, the present center, demographically speaking, is quite a way west even of Shinjuku. Yet the east, the people of the east maintain, *is* Tokyo; always has been, always will be. A few skyscrapers can't change that. Those in a position to know predict Suzuki will have a tough time forcing the scheme through, and will probably fail.

Beyond the conflicts of local interest, one senses a larger, older trend gathering force behind the forces of conservatism, influencing in a vague and incalculable

. . . The light of a summer day fades, the workers disgorge from their offices in the big new buildings into the street, and they all move one way along the broad sidewalk, eastward, into the bowels of Shinjuku Station, which is the largest in the land. It's one of those benign, irresistible Japanese crowds, and if you happened to be standing there, admiring the sunset behind the crazy new skyline, minding your own business, wondering idly where to go next, north, south, east, or west, suddenly you need wonder no more. You go east, with everyone else. The crowd sweeps you away.

The crowd knows best. With Suzuki's hall unbuilt, West Shinjuku lives only by daylight. Some 200,000 people work here, but at night the buildings are empty hulls. The nighttime population numbers six—the priest of Kumano Shrine in the "central park" and his family. The guests of the fancy new hotels step outside at night to sample Shinjuku's famous action—and find themselves in the middle of nowhere.

Everyone's gone east. Their backs to the sunset, they've been sucked into the bright halls and passages of Shinjuku Station, Tokyo's great Palace of the People, megastructure extraordinary, a labyrinth of public and private railway lines, multistory shopping centers topped by floors of restaurants, endless promenades, seedy underground plazas, a station used by two and a half million people every day, home to hundreds of bums, place of assignation for scores of assorted fiends and deviants, yet neither sinister nor dangerous: only impossible. Like the nameless and numberless streets outside, Shinjuku Station, with its monolingual signs, defies the alien to make the foggiest sense of it. And while we blunder back and forth, growing ever more exasperated, two million Japanese flow past with the assurance of sleepwalkers.

On the east side the exit we have picked at random and in desperation spits us out through a basement hall

way how the thing goes: that beacon over there to the east, the Imperial Palace. Perhaps there's still power left in its old embrace.

╫

full of unrecognizable foods, past a McDonald's crowded with teenagers, up stairs, through a florist's shop, and out, into the East Shinjuku dusk.

⌗

Fifteen or more years after it attained its greatest notoriety, Kabuki-cho in East Shinjuku is still Tokyo's greatest *sakariba*, which means "pleasure quarter" but literally translates as "prosperous place." Friday evening: the touts with their tight perms and black jump suits are out on the streets, crouching by the entrances to their peep shows and cop-a-feel parlors; the young girls let out of offices and schools change in the toilet and come tripping down in twos and threes and gangs, in their finery, tight flared pants, and yellow shoes, hobo overcoats, huge earrings, down to the big cinemas and discos and game centers and clubs at the heart of the area—places like the Koma Stadium, the Milano-za, the Disco New York New York, the Cinema Square. They're the first wave, but it's only the beginning and the night will be a long one. Kabuki-cho is only just waking up.

At six the tiny bars on the little lanes in Golden Gai, "Golden Town," are barely reviving. These pleasure zones look their most vulnerable at twilight. "Bright Flower Garden Street the First" is no more than six feet wide. It's all bars on both sides, wooden, two-story terraces. It's still much too early for clients, so the stirrings of life now are unguarded, homely, private. A young child and her granny sit outside on stools while the granny heaps the kid's mouth with noodles. Someone's sweeping up. The alley is cluttered with the belongings of the people who cram their lives into these tiny spaces—plastic dustbins, styrofoam boxes, washing machines, plant pots, bicycles, buckets. The bars are like jewel cases or hat boxes and not much bigger, already glowing like lanterns. A mama-san in her long gown sprawls on a chair behind the bead curtain, her feet in the alley.

The fabled pleasure zone of Yoshiwara over in the east has long had its day, and Kabuki-cho is the capital's new nightless city. What pleasure is overlooked there? What vice uncatered for? All-night bars—all-night saunas—a thousand restaurants—acres of love hotels—peep shows—kinky coffee shops—grilled-chicken stands—*rakugo* story-telling parlors . . .

The place is practically brand-new. Before the war it was just another part of town. Razed in 1945's air raids, it was the fastest to rebuild and recoup, with dozens of little factories and workshops opening up right after the surrender. "Light from Shinjuku" was the section's postwar slogan, but no one bothered to inquire too closely where the fuel came from. Shinjuku was the focus of all the frenetic, seedy life of those hard times, the blackmarketeering, the GI bars and hen houses. Some of that wildness has yet to be tamed.

It was in the '60s that East Shinjuku had its day of glory. Tokyo had its '60s like everywhere else, and unlike other crazes, punk, for example, learned rotefashion from the West, it was a real thing. There was a real sense of liberation in the air. Politically the anti-Vietnam War movement was given local edge by the widespread opposition to the Japan–U.S. Security Treaty, expressed in those massive and stunningly violent student demonstrations at the end of the decade which made it onto the early evening news all over the West. Hippy sympathies were real, too, for the first generation of Japanese youth to grow up rich enough to feel bad about it.

East Shinjuku was the focus of the whole phenomenon, the drugs, the free love, the artistic movements. Everyone who was around then has their favorite East Shinjuku anecdote. In his workshop, a country potter recalls how he camped out there with the hard-core hippies on the station steps while taking a break from bicycling around the country. An English publisher remembers getting snarled up in a violent demo and fleeing from the riot police through a gap in a fence, with a thousand demonstrators hot on his heels.

Something of the spirit of the epoch lingers in Kinokuniya, the famous Shinjuku bookstore, among the smells of coffee and MSG-enriched Japanese curry. It's the barely controlled mayhem of it. Kinokuniya has an excellent theater and thousands and thousands of books, but no refinement. It's an endless hurly-burly.

The elevators are always full, the stairways crowded, the different departments crammed with customers devouring volume after volume without paying (a national vice) under the stark fluorescent tubes, before the nicotine-colored brick-tiled walls. The interior hasn't changed much since Nagisa Oshima shot *Diary of a Shinjuku Thief* here in 1969. It was the most anarchic film of his career.

#

Anarchy is the East Shinjuku style, and it's at its most bizarre and frenzied a few minutes' walk downhill from the Kinokuniya store, in Kabuki-cho's heart. Yet it's not lawless. Like the *yakuza*, the "gangsters" who own and run Kabuki-cho's porno shops and sex rackets, it's beyond the pale of the straight world, but it is held in check by rigid rules and conventions of its own. And those rules are not significantly different from those of mainstream Japanese society. As a result, Kabuki-cho is rough, lurid, noisy, and goes on all night—yet in essentials it's not different from a regular Tokyo main street. It's just a sort of comically exaggerated version of that.

Like the city's more conventional main streets, Kabuki-cho is the creation of a society whose crucial divisions are not those of occupation or class. As Professor Chie Nakane wrote in *Japanese Society*, "The overall picture of society is not that of horizontal stratification by class but of vertical stratification by institution or group of institutions." This brings about "numerous vertical schisms" in the society. The modern Japanese cityscape provides a perfect illustration. Building materials and techniques, the "diet" of the Japanese architect, grow more and more Western; yet the aesthetic values which, in the West, determine the way those materials are used, refuse to take root. The reason is that they are the creation of societies whose important divisions are horizontal ones.

The rigid adherence to street lines in a city like New York—the almost moral revulsion exhibited by someone like *New York Times* architectural critic Paul Goldberger when they are violated—is a twentieth-century expression of those divisions, just as the crescents and terraces of a city like Bath in England are eighteenth-century ones. The harmonious and orderly alignment of equals, whether modern corporate headquarters or the town houses of a bygone ruling class, is one of the greatest charms of a Western city. It's a charm which Tokyo strikingly lacks—and perhaps it's this, even more than the curving orientation of the city's streets to the beacon of the Imperial Palace, which is the fundamental reason behind the lack of "urban scenic beauty" lamented by Kazuhiro Ishii.

For in Japan's increasingly egalitarian society, in which, nonetheless, nobody is actually equal to anybody else—not even pairs of identical twins—harmony of the Western sort cannot come to pass. In its place is the intense yet rigidly controlled rivalry graphically illustrated in the narrow and smelly backstreets of Kabuki-cho.

It's a sort of polar opposite of harmony. You can see the steps that have been taken to reach the present state of things. Two shops in the same line of business set up next door to each other—peep show plus "adult toys," for the sake of argument. Both hang up signs. A takes the sign in, repaints it in bigger letters, B responds in kind. Light bulbs are hung around the edge of the sign, then neon. Escalation: next a sign goes out on the street and loudspeakers are wired up to the entrance, to blare forth *Irasshai, irasshai!* ("Welcome, welcome!") and a little ditty around the clock. The sign's torn down, up goes another, this time twice as big as the building to which it's attached. . . .

This process, repeated up and down every alley, results in the typical Kabuki-cho street scene, and through this tunnel of light and noise the punter gropes his way, blinded and deafened, a barely sensible lump of meat almost taken in hand and physically massaged by the sensory assault. Yet Kabuki-cho only takes to absurdity what is quite a normal feature of the Japanese cityscape, and, beyond the realm of architecture, of the whole culture. Toyota and Nissan, Sony and National Panasonic, the *Asahi* and *Mainichi* newspapers, all have the same sort of relationship of bitter and furious rivalry as the Kabuki-cho peep shows. And these are the society's most fundamental divisions.

Classical harmony is consequently beyond the scope of Japanese architects, but in its place they have the possibility of developing an architecture of radical originality. Wealthy, sophisticated, superabundantly supplied with information from all over the world, they have the chance to create forms which, because they faithfully reflect a unique social structure, are unlike anything yet seen on the face of the earth.

Most of the time, unfortunately, they botch it. As in West Shinjuku they put up clones of Skidmore, Owings & Merrill, of Philip Johnson, of anything that's fashionable, and then the dynamic of their own society finds expression only in negative ways; in a pathetic absence of harmony between buildings which, because the forms are Western, *demand* to be harmonized; in the inane shapelessness, for example, of the spaces between the West Shinjuku skyscrapers.

But occasionally, in the odd building, an architect of brilliance realizes the potential. East Shinjuku has at least one such. It's a bar building in the heart of Kabuki-cho called Ichibankan. Minoru Takeyama designed it when he returned to Japan in the late '60s after six years abroad.

"When I came back, so much of Tokyo had changed," he told me, "all the places I had been familiar with. Only this part of Shinjuku seemed still to have the atmosphere that I remembered. It made me nostalgic. I designed Ichibankan in that sort of mood."

The section of Kabuki-cho it stands in is full of these bar buildings, structures of five or six or more stories crammed with small pubs, clubs, and "snacks" from top to bottom, separated by inches and singlemindedly devoted to shouting each other down. Ichibankan has forty-nine bars, yes forty-nine, distributed through eight floors, and joins in the scrummage in deadly earnest. The difference is that, whereas the others are merely streetwise, Ichibankan is intelligent, too. Takeyama has looked hard and long at what his building must do, and what it need not bother to do, and the result is genuinely original.

First of all, the building must make a splash. It absolutely must not merge into its surroundings. It must shout its head off. Takeyama achieves this with a zebra-striped form clad in iron and glass which looks like an exercise in avant-garde origami.

The rival bar buildings on either side have conventional entrance foyers and elevator halls, like low-rent office buildings. Why bother? What boozer wants to be reminded of his workplace? In function a bar building like this is essentially an up-ended Golden Gai alley, like the one we passed through earlier as it was waking up. As in Golden Gai, all the snugness and luxury is inside the individual bars; outside is outside, whether it's the

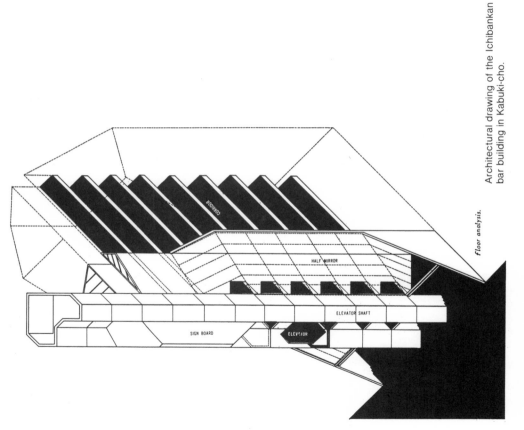

floor analysis.

CORRIDOR

HALF MIRROR

ELEVATOR SHAFT

SIGN BOARD

ELEVATOR

Architectural drawing of the Ichibankan bar building in Kabuki-cho.

street or eight floors up, and thus Ichibankan has an aperture rather than an entrance, and no front door. Squeeze in, stroll up. The huge areas of window on either side of the elevators help to reinforce the sensation that this is a street in the air.

Finally, there's the treatment of the signs. The bars are the raison d'être of these buildings, and accordingly the signs advertising them ought to be the focus of attention; yet on most of the nearby buildings they seem to have been stuck on just anyhow, as afterthoughts. At Ichibankan, they fit snugly into the gap between the two structural columns at the front, and the chevrons of the windows rush down towards them like diving birds. They are the center of the design, all the rest converges on them.

There are streaks of rust down Ichibankan's walls now, and the name's peeling off; unlike Takeyama's equally extraordinary Nibankan nearby, which recently emerged in glory from a respray, it has not been kept up. But Takeyama was not designing for posterity, or for the steely gaze of the academician. Unlike some of the pop dabblings of American architects, his work is sincere in the favored Japanese sense: it's 100 percent committed to its role. There is no patrician sniggering behind the punter's back.

The building's slight dilapidation is a reminder of another characteristic of Japanese architecture which has both negative and positive aspects: its ephemerality. As was mentioned in the discussion of the shita-machi earlier, the capital's traditional wooden houses had a lifetime of only a generation or two, and rebuilding was the householder's routine duty. The idea of "permanent" buildings only came in with Westernization, and it's still an alien one. But in this respect the West may, without direct imitation, be coming around to the East's traditional way of seeing things, as rapidly changing technology means that more and more buildings exhaust their usefulness in decades rather than centuries. And in Japan, too, the traditional attitude has recently begun to be reexamined to see if it has anything to offer the present age.

A phrase which has gained wide currency as a pointer

to new trends in design and industry is *keihaku tansho*. Literally translating somewhat pejoratively as "frivolous and petty," the four characters by which the words are written are *kei* (lightweight), *haku* (skin-deep), *tan* (short), and *sho* (small). Taken together they identify the key elements of many of the new products by which Japan has prospered in recent years, from the transistor radio to the Walkman, from the miniature scooter to the capsule hotel.

They also help us to appreciate what is lively and different about Japan's new architecture—or so Takeyama believes. His own Ichibankan is one of the best demonstrations of the theory.

Heaviness, thickness, great tortoiselike longevity, massive size: these have been the prerequisites of architectural respectability in the West from Stonehenge to Michael Graves. Ever since the Meiji Restoration of 1868, Japan's architects have been dutifully grafting these stony Western blooms onto the native stem, but skepticism and anarchy, frivolity and pettiness have always been erupting in the grass roots. Architecture can be fun! And it needn't last forever! Come and see!

⧻

One of the merits of frivolity and pettiness is that it gives the city's form a flexibility, a sensitivity to the changing demands of its people, which cannot be matched by a city clad in stone.

Kabuki-cho is a case in point: after centuries of being nowhere special, it was suddenly, at the end of the war, in just the right place: at a center of transportation in the quarter of the city which was receiving an enormous influx of new people. Kabuki-cho had no tradition; and practically the only structure still left standing after the air raids was the elevated railway. All it had was a hungry energy. But shrewdly and intelligently channeled, that was enough to make of it the most prosperous and dynamic sakariba in the whole city.

It is hard to imagine such a thing happening in a Western city, where the hegemony of the traditional center, symbolized by its historic buildings, is hardly usurped without a struggle. In Europe, old buildings are treated with such respect that someone from a different part of the world might reasonably interpret them as the objects of a local cult of ancestor worship. Like the cows of India, many of them are inviolate, no matter how inconvenient they have become, how remote from contemporary needs. Social life revolves around them, magnetically attracted by the charisma of age. London's Covent Garden Market was an old neoclassical building which housed a fruit and vegetable market. When the market was rehoused elsewhere, there was a plan to tear the building down, which was fiercely and successfully resisted. And wisely resisted, as it turned out, for the shopping and dining center it has since become the focus of is undoubtedly the most flourishing sakariba in London. It's hardly a convenient spot, the nearest tube station is small, dingy, and ill-served; the market building, however, is marvelously old and atmospheric. That was what mattered most.

In Japan there is no tradition of according respect to buildings on account of their age. If the values which they incarnate cannot be re-created in our own lives, the thought goes, and find equally beautiful forms of expression in our own time and through our own hands, then the building is no more than a monument to our degeneracy, measuring the distance we have fallen. Let it rot.

Tokyo has had a few solid buildings of worth in its time, and as a result of this attitude they have nearly all gone under the wrecker's ball. The saddest case was the demolition of Frank Lloyd Wright's magnificent Imperial Hotel, the second Imperial, completed in 1923 and torn down in 1967. Even then it lasted thirty years longer than it would have if the owners had had their way: they originally planned to get rid of it in 1937 so they could put up something more practical in time for the (later aborted) Tokyo Olympics of 1940. To their credit, many Japanese architects put up a strong resistance to the owners' various schemes. Among laymen, however, even those who loved it for its "sorcerer's castle" atmosphere, the common reaction was, what's the fuss? Buildings aren't meant to last forever, are they?

The sakariba of Tokyo require no fine buildings to lure the punters; a few noisy shacks are enough. As a result, places like Kabuki-cho burst into flower practically overnight. And Kabuki-cho is only the most famous. As Tokyo's population swelled and the city bulged further and further beyond its old limits, more and more minor halts became major stations, more and more unimportant crossroads became huge intersections, more and more thirsty workers and students disgorged on the streets eager to drop into anywhere welcoming for a quick one or three before the last leg home. This was the process, and whenever a certain critical state was reached, another minor halt, another fork in the road had become a major sakariba. Nothing else is needed—no squares or plazas—the alley is cozier; no intimations of history or tradition—there are plenty of carpenters who can cobble together the likeness of a country farmhouse or an English pub for those who want atmosphere. All you need are trains and crowds; all you need is mass thirst, and a few people canny enough to see the sense in catering to it.

Shinjuku, Ikebukuro, Shibuya on the west side of the loop; Nakano, Koenji, Kichijoji on the Chuo Line going out beyond; dozens of smaller spots in between, and bigger ones further on and out: all over the map they light up like candles, each with its rows of red lanterns hung outside, its smells of barbecuing chicken, soy sauce, cheap saké, and roasting chestnuts, clouds of smoke, huddles of office workers and laborers and tradesmen and students hunkered down on beer crates, yelling at each other over the roaring of the trains.

All the sakariba look pretty much the same, but oddly they're all quite different: each brews a special character from its own unique mix of residents and passers-through. Ikebukuro, north and west of Shinjuku on the loop, has a raw, bumpkin quality, thanks to the farmers who come through on their way in from the wilds of Saitama Prefecture. Shibuya and Harajuku, to the south of Shinjuku, are young, girlish, full of fashion stores. Kichijoji's full of jazzmen, and Shimo-kitazawa, a bit to the south and west, is good for theater. Roppongi, inside the loop, breaks the pattern because it's relative-

Bars under the railway arches at Yuraku-cho in central Tokyo. ▲

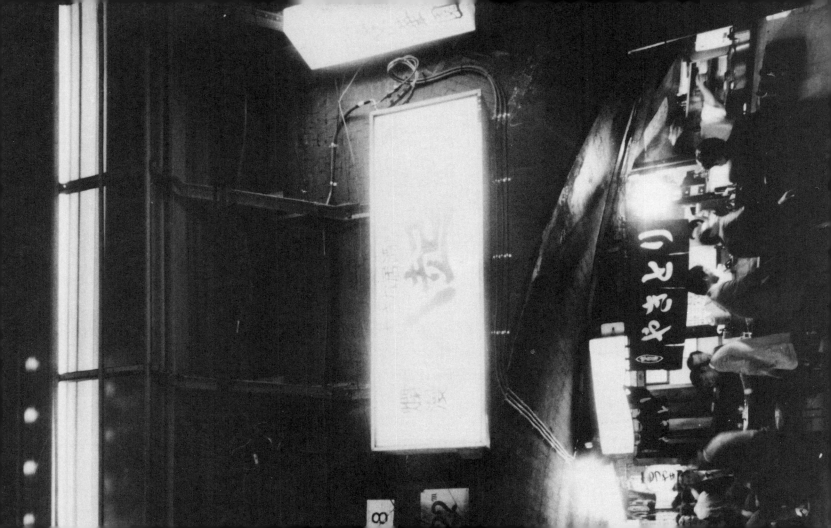

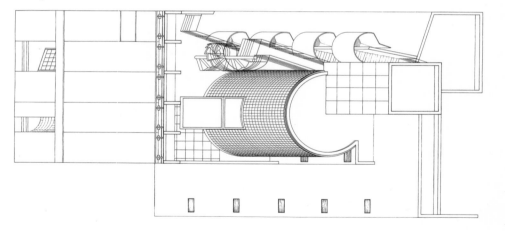

Glass Art Akasaka, a new bar building designed by Arata Isozaki.

ly hard to get to, being located on a single subway line, so it's the one for the inner-city kids, the local foreigners, and the people with cars.

The reputations of sakariba are made and broken from year to year. Kichijoji and Shimo-kitazawa are pretty new; Kabuki-cho's looking a little haggard; Roppongi shows early signs of giving way to neighboring Hiroo.

In *The City in History* Lewis Mumford, the great apostle of urban planning, defines with his customary rotundity "the essential facilities and functions of the city" as "cooperation, communication, and communion, meeting, mixture, and mobilization." Nobody ever planned a sakariba, at least not one that worked; "they just growed." Yet in a way that Mumford would undoubtedly have found frivolous and aesthetically unedifying, they do what he says a city should. They are where the city is most alive.

And they add a new dimension of complexity to the picture of a "strong center" city, its population focused like mesmerized insects on the beacon of the Imperial Palace, which we entertained earlier. The truth of that picture is in any case very limited. With its implicit authoritarianism and its clarity of structure, that image sounds like the work of a Mussolini. Yet one thing anyone who has looked hard at Japan realizes before long is that integration in the classical sense is a quality the Japanese are happy to get along without. As architect and Tokyo University professor Fumihiko Maki explains, Tokyo since the earliest times has accommodated several quite different and apparently contradictory morphological principles.

"Besides the radial streets coming out of the center and the spiral of moats," he said, "there was the city's orientation to major mountain, river, and road, which was based on Chinese ideas. Downtown in the old merchant's center of Nihombashi you find a grid plan, but always with a limit to it; it didn't extend throughout. Elsewhere you have whole sections oriented around a view of Mount Fuji or Mount Tsukuba.

"'In this way there are five, six, or seven different morphological principles at work in the city. Tokyo was never a geometrical, abstract city like ancient Athens or modern New York.

"When the Meiji period came, Westerners gave a certain influence to the making of the city, but again it was always only up to a point. There was Omotesando, for example, and Gaien Higashi-dori, two broad, tree-lined, boulevard-like streets—but only those two. They just end there. Then after the war we brought in the expressway system, which again is an absolutely different sort of notion. . . . So there is no totality in modern Tokyo.''

It's the smashing of the Western city's historical totality by the expressway and the skyscraper which is so upsetting to many Western commentators, and which seems to them such an augury of barbarism. If this ancient city, Tokyo, seems to accommodate them with less fuss, one reason may be that there is no totality to smash.

Maki calls Tokyo a "collage of different ideas and principles." "I see it as a net in which are snarled like brightly colored fish a thousand different worlds—West Shinjuku's Manhattan, Golden Gai's hatbox bars, French boulevards, expressways, Ginza's glittering stores, mountain views, the nine-hole wilderness in the middle, the lights of the sakariba breaking out across the plain. . . ."

5

THE ENCHANTED CASTLE

We are in a cave and something terrifying and magnificent is happening, but we are not alarmed. We are oddly cool. Coolly we have the whole thing framed and focused in the viewfinder of our excellent Japanese camera.

We are at the back of a high, arching cave with boulders, jagged ledges, and stalactites, illuminated by a rich bronze light. But beyond, down there, the cave's ragged walls and arches are replaced by the soaring columns, the clerestory, and the fan-vaulting of a Gothic cathedral. The light is the same, and its source is the eruption that is taking place in the cathedral's transept, where a Saturn rocket has just blasted off, leaving a blinding gout of incandescence and gasoline flame which consumes the bank of pews, and drives a clutch of terrified, half-naked men to the cave walls. Where the tip of the rocket points skyward white sunlight pours in, drenching the fan-vaulting, bestowing on the capsule—are there people in there?—a blinding aureola.

The work is a photomontage by Tsunehisa Kimura, the man introduced in chapter 1 who saw Osaka burn. Like much of his work, the image is in roughly equal parts glamorous and sinister: there is erotic fascination in the treatment of the jagged rock, the cruel, carved

The Hegemony, photo-
montage by Tsunehisa
Kimura, 1978.

stone, and wrought iron, the soaring, man-dwarfing height of the whole composition. But at a deeper level there is fascination with the fact that cave, cathedral, and rocket form a continuum—a continuum remote from Japan's own culture at every point

It's a brand of fascination which breaks out all over the place in Japan's contemporary culture. Contemplating the West and its works, the long tradition which led from the stone monument to the moon rocket, and which Japan has devoted a century and a little bit to becoming part of, the Japanese is bound to feel a complex emotion. Revulsion and attraction, horror and wonder are sensed in such close succession that they practically fuse; horror-struck anticipation of what may be suffered—"No More Hiroshimas"—alternates with delighted anticipation of what may be achieved.

And mixed in with it is a different anxiety. For having achieved what there is to achieve, what will they have become? What if the man in that capsule, perched at the pinnacle of ten thousand years of alien culture and headed for the moon, were Japanese? What would be Japanese about him by the time he got back?

Since the Meiji Restoration, Japan has been buying into Western civilization like no other non-Western nation before or since. From an early date the nation's rulers seem to have understood that as part of that process, part of the deal, the people would have to change. But how much? How deeply? Isolated for centuries from the bewildering mirrors of the outside world, the Japanese had preserved to a great extent what Germain Bazin in *The Baroque*, speaking of medieval European man, calls "That sense of continuity between the psyche, nature and the supernatural world which is characteristic of all primitive civilizations." By admitting the West as a model for emulation, the Japanese admitted rationalism; admitting rationalism, they also allowed to be smuggled in "the split," in Bazin's words, which "grew insidiously with the development of reason," "the disruption of the unity of the civilized world which occurred at the time of the Renaissance."

"... The men of the seventeenth and eighteenth centuries," Bazin goes on, "withdrew from their inner conflicts by living on two planes at once, one real and one imaginary. Perhaps the most surprising feature of baroque art ... is how men who in thought and deed created new worlds could indulge in childish games of make-believe. One might pretend to be Apollo, Rinaldo the Grand Turk, or even Confucius, but never simply oneself: as if the art of living consisted in flight from the self ... the idea was put forward that one might even disguise oneself as oneself.''

A century and more later on the other side of the world, conditions were very different, but the throwing into doubt of what had previously been taken for granted was the same; similar, too, was the urge to flee from oneself—whatever *that* might be—into a dreamland of different disguises, not the least splendid of which was the disguise known as ''Japanese.''

Tokyo was the stage for this confusing new epoch. As, during the course of a century, the myriad different costumes were tried on and discarded—English gentleman, Ali Baba, Yankee big shot, Spanish grandee, astronaut, E.T., not to mention the infinite variations on the theme ''Japanese''—the city came more and more to resemble the back-lot of the world's biggest movie studio. That's the way things stand today.

⊞

At the beginning, perhaps, after the coming of Commodore Perry's ships in 1853, no danger was perceived. To win the respect of the powerful foreigner, and to persuade him to repeal the odious treaties the Japanese had been forced to sign, which gave the foreigner rights of extraterritoriality, it was deemed wise to adopt the outward show of his civilization. The emperor sprouted whiskers, wore a braided jacket with epaulettes, half-sat, half-slouched in an armchair, ate beef. The military and the government bureaucracy adopted Western-style uniforms. But these were merely prudent and pragmatic manipulations of the surface. The earliest Western-style buildings in Japan were built by Japanese carpenters who ingeniously reproduced in wood the proportions and surface decorations their clients required; the structure within was a traditional one of posts and

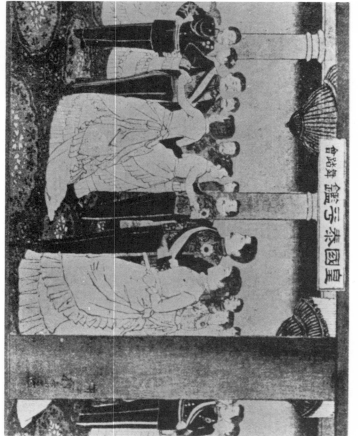

Contemporary print of Japanese couples dancing at the Rokumeikan in the 1880s.

beams. The Westernization of dress and custom was superficial in much the same way. And like the new-style building's posts and beams, the man within the *moningu* ("morning coat") remained stolidly Japanese.

It's interesting that it was after the construction of one of the first thoroughgoing Western buildings in the city—Western to the marrow—that intellectual Japanese first began to give indications that they were lurching into something rather deeper than they had bargained for, something over which they might not be able to retain complete control.

The building was called the Rokumeikan, and it was erected to the designs of an English architect resident in Japan, Josiah Conder, between 1881 and 1883. It was a state-owned lodging house and gathering-place where foreigners and high-ranking Japanese could meet socially. It was considered so significant for the city's development that the years of its glory came to be known as the "Rokumeikan era."

Edward G. Seidensticker has provided a detailed account of the building and what went on inside it in *Low City, High City*. "It was a two-storey structure of brick," he writes, "in an Italianate style most splendid for the time, with about fifteen thousand square feet of floor space. It had a ballroom, a music room, a billiard room, a reading room, suites for illustrious guests, and a bathtub such as had never before been seen in the land: alabaster, six feet long and three feet wide. Water thundered most marvelously, we are told, from the faucets."

Westernization was a show and the Rokumeikan was a showplace, but like the uncompromising brick structure of the building, the show as staged here was taken to extremes of fidelity to the original never before attempted. Invitations were addressed jointly to husbands and wives. The orchestra kept European hours, playing till long after the rest of the city was asleep. The events staged were purely and exclusively European ones—garden parties, evening receptions, a charity bazaar. "Whether done easily or not," Professor Seidensticker tells us, "dancing was the main thing to do at the Rokumeikan. Ladies and gentlemen were expected to appear in foreign dress. . . . Beginning late in 1884, ladies and gentlemen gathered for regular and studiously organized practice in the waltz, the quadrille, and the like."

Before the end of the decade, as a result of a political scandal and renewed outrage over extraterritoriality, the Rokumeikan's day was done, and the high tide of Meiji Westernization had passed. But as Seidensticker indicates elsewhere in the same book, it left its mark on the Japanese psyche. "The literature known as modern, with its beginnings in the Rokumeikan decade, the 1880s, is obsessively, gnawingly intellectual," he writes. "If a single theme runs through it, that theme is the quest for identity, an insistence upon what it is that establishes the individual as individual."

At some point in that all-too-convincing foreign pantomime, the Japanese had lost their certainty; somewhere, among the "myriads of little lights" on the opening night, on the great staircase "solidly embanked with chrysanthemums," or on the dance floor, while stiffly but closely entwined with some foreign personage—

perhaps sensing in alarm that one might be beginning to enjoy it—the seed of doubt had been sown. The question. "Who am I?"—unaskable and absurd yesterday—was all of a sudden the only one that mattered.

⊹

Sometimes these days in Tokyo you can see lovers holding hands. Even on the trains they do it, "shamelessly." Some of them are even in school uniform. But it's still a rare enough thing to turn heads and provoke old-fashioned looks. When I see a young couple who are obviously fond of each other I find myself thinking, oh, so Japan has lovers, too. Japan has love, too.

It's still much more common for them to stay out of sight. Japan's lovers have traditionally behaved with the furtiveness of an oppressed and despised minority. But just as they have gingerly begun "coming out," so in the past two decades have they come to be provided with places of refuge appropriate to their numerical and economic strength: the love hotels.

⊹

Vulnerability seems to be the permanent condition of true love in Japan. Marriage was until very recent times seen as a liaison between families rather than individuals. Within marriage, love was an improbable and scarcely significant side-effect. Outside, it was something subversive, a threat to the established and profitable way of doing things, and its routine fate was either to be dissolved in an access of realism, or to be crushed. Among the most poignant works in the whole of Japanese literature are the "love suicide" plays written around the turn of the eighteenth century by Chikamatsu Monzaemon for the Bunraku puppet theater. In a play of this genre, a pair of hopeless and usually quite hapless lovers, a high-class geisha and an apprentice soy-sauce dealer, say, or flour merchant, recognize after successive contortions of plot that their love is doomed. They then travel to somewhere poetical such as the wood of Sonezaki or the strand at Amijima—the long-drawn-out last journey is always the best and saddest bit—there to end it all.

These plays were often based on real incidents, which was one of the reasons for their great popularity. Likewise lifted from a news story was the plot of *Ai no Coriida* (*The Empire of the Senses*), film director Nagisa Oshima's famous erotic masterpiece, made in 1978, about the monomaniacal love between an innkeeper and a prostitute, which culminates in the woman strangling the man (with his consent) to obtain one final orgasm, then cutting off his member as a keepsake.

The real events that inspired *Ai no Coriida* took place earlier this century, the tragedies dramatized by Chikamatsu more than 200 years earlier. Yet the claustrophobic intensity of the love relationship, and the sense that the lovers have willfully divorced themselves from social realities which will crush their relationship if they can, are the same in both. "The power of *Ai no Coriida*," Oshima told me when I interviewed him a couple of years ago, "derives from the fact that the eroticism which is its subject is something purely Japanese, unaffected by any foreign influence whatsoever."

In Japanese love, vulnerability is the constant, death frequently the price to be paid. This is the almost unchanging historical background, and set against it the love hotel, that amazing product of Japan's contemporary culture, which was copied from nowhere and has no close equivalent anywhere in the world, may become a little easier to understand.

Because for many non-Japanese there's something distinctly ludicrous about the whole phenomenon. And for all the gadgets and appliances with which its rooms are equipped, and by which its worldwide fame has been assured, it's not even erotic. For non-Japanese, it's a turn-off.

"If soft music, candlelight and a bottle of wine are your idea of a romantic setting," wrote UPI correspondent in Tokyo Todd Eastham, "the Hotel Meguro Emperor probably is not your kind of place. But if circular beds that vibrate, undulate and ascend into mirrored sanctums replete with artificial moonlight tickle your fancy, long nights of unbridled titillation await you there."

Ann Nakano of Tokyo's English-language *Mainichi Daily News* went to the same hotel—it's said to be the biggest and best in town, and it's certainly the most popular with the foreign press corps—and found to her distress that the amazing equipment did more to dissipate than concentrate her partner's energies.

A recent visit . . . purely for investigational purposes I may add, revealed what I had long suspected: there are so many gadgets and good things to play with . . . that it is difficult to concentrate on one's partner. . . .

. . . Leading to the bath is what appears to be the world's most perfect slide. Fun and games. You can get quite carried away lurching down one of those things into the warm, luxurious, foamy white bubble bath. . . .

From inside the bedroom you can watch your partner laze in the bath, or you can yell at him to stop whizzing down that damn slide and get the hell in here. Take your pick. . . .

The worst thing of all, in my opinion, is the darn *karaoke* machine [literally, "empty orchestra"—sing-along music tapes with a microphone]. I suggest you skip this. There's nothing that turns a girl off more than a young chap sitting on the end of her circular bed loudly belting out "You are my sunshine," especially when he doesn't know the words. . . ."

My advice is, if you're with a hot new date, then book yourselves into one of the bigger, better [i.e., conventional] hotels. This way you'll keep your mind on the job.

Candlelight, soft music, a bottle of wine, a table for two . . . that's the sort of ambience a Western romance prospers in. It's the essence of taste, simplicity, openness. They order these things quite otherwise in Tokyo.

Wherever you have come from, you go, when you are ready, or when you can persuade her, to a special section of town. It is an amazing and uncanny place. The hotels are mostly huge, ungainly piles, rising sheer from the street four, six, eight, even ten stories high. They have classical columns and capitals. They have bulging balconies with pilasters. They have stone or plaster statues of naked ladies in graceful postures. They have coats of arms, mansard roofs, dormer windows, spires, turrets, cornices—every cliché in the European ar-

▼ Hotel Meguro Emperor at sunset.

chitectural book. Everything architectural spare parts can do to create the impression that we are beyond everyday life, in fairyland, never-never land, has been done.

Most striking of all is how many of these hotels have battlements. The Meguro Emperor, "king of love hotels," is the best specimen, because it's really quite a loving copy of one of Prince Ludwig's Bavarian flights of fancy. Another, the Tenshukaku, in a "love zone" way out on one of the expressways, is an equally faithful copy of an old Japanese donjon. Toride, another expressway hotel, is a huge blow-up of a toy-town fort. Others treat the theme more lightly (and cheaply), tacking aluminum or plaster battlements onto the standard concrete hulk, throwing in a turret or a keep. But there are certainly plenty of them.

The same preoccupation is reflected in the hotels' names, more than half of which are English or other foreign borrowings. A few have a suggestion of frivolity, fun, or style about them—"Charme," "Dream," "Edelweiss," "Elegance," or, veering towards the ludicrous, "Moomin." Several, including some of the most recently opened, have pinched European trade names—"Dunhill," "Chanel," "Perrier," "Air France." But what is again striking is how many of the hotels (including several which have no battlements) choose names expressive of strength and protectiveness: "Giant," "Highness," "Guard," "Castelle," "Chateau," "Ojo" ("King's Castle"), "Blue Castle," "Emperor" . . . Japan's young lovers feel as vulnerable as ever, it seems. The surest way to lure them in is to assure them that once inside they will be totally safe.

The streets of the love-hotel zone have a special weird beauty at twilight, after the hotels have put their lights on but before it's fully dark. All the big hotels here are adrip with neon, with flashing signs, nameboards that light up one letter at a time, zipping dotted arrows—but the streets of the zone are quite deserted, with the exception of the odd couple scurrying away; and utterly quiet. . . . It's an odd, lonely feeling, all this big-city brightness for no one.

The procedure is this: you pick your hotel, either by

roaming the streets till you come to one you fancy, or by consulting a guidebook, or you go to one which you have been to before. If you are driving you duck your car down the driveway into the underground garage which all the big places have these days, the entranceway masked by strips of vinyl. If you're on foot you step around the screening walls and into the lobby. On the wall there, if the hotel is one which has any pretensions, will be an illuminated plexiglass panel with colored photographs of the rooms and their names, numbers, and prices. The cheapest have the bare essentials—a vast drum-shaped bed, a sofa, a stereo, a color TV with a special porno channel, an elaborate bathroom. The pricier ones have a host of extra gimmicks, some of which have been mentioned already. There are beds which go up and down or rotate, beds embedded in Rolls Royces or pianos or Queen Elizabeth's coronation coach. Some of the rooms come with swimming pools or saunas, many with sado-masochist equipment. One famous hotel, the Alpha-In, which is overlooked by the patrician American Club and the Soviet Embassy, has S-M gear in every room.

A normal Western reaction to a love-hotel room, whether it's groaning with chains and whips or not, is to squirm, whereas this is obviously not true of the Japanese. If it were, it is hardly likely that fifty-five million couples in the Tokyo area alone would make use of love hotels in a single year. And yet in 1982, we are assured, that is the number that did.

I believe a simple cultural difference underlies these radically different reactions.

The first thing a Westerner is reminded of on entering a room in a love hotel is his or her own bedroom. It's a grotesque vulgarization and distortion of that. The Western bedroom is a private place, the one room in the house visitors almost never see. What takes place in a bedroom is correspondingly private and intimate—and in this context the love-hotel room is far too up-front.

The average Japanese, on the other hand, is not reminded of his bedroom because he doesn't have one; he has only a tatami-matted room, used as a living room during the day, in which his futon and that of his wife, and very commonly those of their small children, too, are spread out at night. So the Japanese association is not with a bedroom, with its particular memories of intimacy, but with the room of a regular Western-style hotel.

This means something very different. Its associations are affluence, foreign travel, shamelessness (the Japanese have a proverb, "The traveler leaves his shame at home"), exotic pleasure—freedom of every sort, and perhaps especially the freedom of being able to experiment, in a foreign country, away from the constricting expectations of Japanese society, with a fresh idea of who one is.

The vulgar explicitness of the term "love hotel," and the fact that fifty-five million couples in or near the capital visit them in a single year, may leave one with the impression of a nation preoccupied with sex to an amazing degree. This I think is wrong. A visit to a love hotel does not have to be the steamy climax to a seduction or the secret consummation of a private affair. As a practical Japanese-language guide to the subject suggests, a couple of student friends might take advantage of the cheap daytime rates to study or to watch baseball on the big-screen TV. Many married couples undoubtedly use them as places to relax for a few hours away from children and in-laws. Sex may not even take place; lacking the puritanical sense that sex is sinful, Japanese tend to invest it with less make-or-break significance. The favored term for the new, more sophisticated, less garish establishments that have been opening up in the past couple of years is "leisure hotel," which may give a more rounded idea of their purpose.

So when you've studied the photographs on the wall and made up your mind about what sort of room you fancy or which you can afford, you can tell the clerk quite freely and openly, even if it's the most elaborate S-M room in the building. Shame has no place here. After all, maybe all you want is a bath and a giggle.

And yet—if that's the case, the reception arrangements seem odd. There's no front desk, no smiling clerk or eager bellhop. You receive your key and later hand over your money at a booth like a box office in a movie theater, with the difference that only the clerk's hands are visible. Neither staff nor clients need ever see each other's faces. And you never sign a book—not even with a false name.

Within the love hotel, anonymity is total: the management does not regard it as their business to know who you are. And that's part of what, for a Japanese, is liberating about the love hotel, because your identity is something you leave outside. Once within the battlements, you have no name or status to weigh you down; in these fantastic surroundings you can flit, a liberated spirit, from one exotic disguise to another, with total irresponsibility; or you can simply collapse and slump back with the huge relief of being nobody special at all for a spell, in this charming and ridiculous noplace.

The Japanese began worrying about their identity a century ago, we learn, in the Rokumeikan decade, and they've been worrying themselves sick about it ever since. The love hotel is one place they can shake it all off.

#

But it's a recourse which has not been available to them for very long. The history of the love hotel goes back barely twenty years.

For hundreds of years, lovers needing to be alone together have resorted to the sort of traditional Japanese inn, or *ryokan*, in which the couple in *Ai no Corrida* spent nearly all their time. The value of such a place as a refuge from society was, however, purely symbolic. Exterior walls of flimsy wood and interior room dividers of stiffened paper meant that true privacy was out of the question. In such a building, the shutting out of the world required an immense psychic effort, intense concentration on the loved one to the exclusion of everything else. This was what helped give the relationship of the lovers in Oshima's film its fatally high voltage.

After the last war, ryokan which specialized in welcoming "guests without baggage" came to be called *tsurekomi ryokan*, or "drag-her-in inns." Ryokan of this type still exist in abundance, catering to those (like many of the city's prostitutes and their clients) who do not demand any special atmosphere. But from the *tsurekomi ryokan* to the love hotel was a quantum leap.

For the development of the love hotel there were three necessary preconditions: capital sufficient to build in concrete—concrete being vital for the hotel's real as well as symbolic privacy; a clientele affluent enough to pay something approaching the night rate of a decent conventional hotel for an hour or two's fun; and, in the minds of the potential clientele, curiosity and appetite, reawakened after the bitterness of defeat and occupation, for the great world beyond the seas.

These three came together in the most crucial year of Japan's postwar history: 1964, the year of the Tokyo Olympics. In that year the economy was beginning its long boom, and ordinary people had money in their pockets. The first Olympics ever to be held in Asia was like Japan getting married to the world all over again. It was in this great year that the construction of Tokyo's first real love hotels got underway.

Eighty years after the opening of the Rokumeikan, with its neoclassical columns and arches and entablature, its decorative eaves and chimneys and its roof crowned with spiky wrought-iron whimsy, new images of foreign opulence and fantasy began sprouting up across the city. But if the scale was grander and the fantasy wilder, the ambition was more modest: not intercourse with the outside world, but the consummation, in surroundings that permitted the imagination to roam, of purely Japanese relationships.

For this most chronically insular of nations, it looks like a step backward.

6
IMAGES OF JAPAN

In another of Tsunehisa Kimura's extraordinary photomontages, two helicopters fly over a typically ugly and disorderly section of central Tokyo, with the Eiffel-like Tokyo Tower at one side of the picture and the grayly bureaucratic Kasumigaseki skyscraper at the other. Suspended between the helicopters is a vast Japanese flag, thousands of square feet in area. There's no other way to tell which country you're in, the implication seems to run. Certainly the architecture won't help you.

It's quite true. In Tokyo, as to a greater or lesser extent in every modern city, the effect of the adoption of Western technology has been the watering down of peculiarly local or national features of the cityscape. Sometimes, as in most of Tokyo, they disappear altogether.

Yet in Tokyo, where, ever since the building with Japanese government money of that foreign monument, the Rokumeikan, the question of national identity has been such a pressing, needling issue, something else happens too. National prestige requires that the organs of state be represented by the most advanced and the most advanced-looking buildings obtainable—which is to say, Western-style. Yet early on in the process of

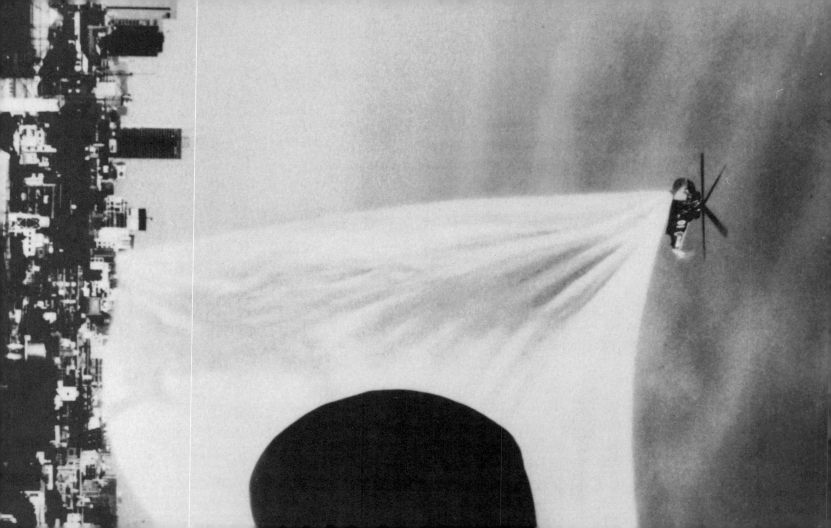

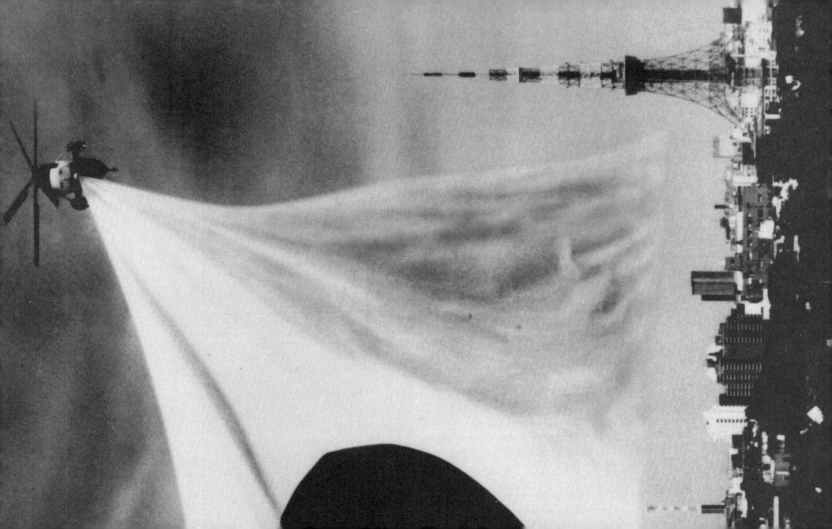

modernization it occurred to the Japanese that they needn't merely be slavish copies, as the Rokumeikan was, of the buildings of Europe; with ingenuity they might be endowed with specifically Japanese qualities and meanings.

This was a new idea, and a brilliant one; its realization was to become one of the most important and seminal currents in the modern architecture of the world. Its expressions in Tokyo are very varied; they constitute a fascinating catalog of the different conclusions those imaginative artists, the architects, reached when they set to pondering on the collective self.

The first example is perhaps the most subtle. In 1890, the year after the Rokumeikan closed down, the Mitsubishi Company bought from the army a broad strip of land bordering the east side of the Imperial Palace. The area was called Marunouchi. Here Mitsubishi established one of the nation's first concentrations of modern office buildings, the Mitsubishi Londontown as it came to be called. The designer of some of the buildings was the same Englishman, Josiah Conder, who had been responsible for the Rokumeikan. The final effect of this later work, however, was to be rather different.

The new section, rising on land that had been little better than wilderness at the time of the purchase, was terrifically impressive. The tall, solid, dignified red-brick buildings rose in neat lines on either side of enormously broad, straight avenues which divided the area in the form of a grid. Both in plan and in detail, nothing could have been more different than the city's traditional face. Yet when, decades later, the whole section was completed, it looked distinctly Japanese—in a way that nothing in history had ever looked Japanese before.

The crucial building, keystone of the whole design, was the red-brick, Dutch-style Tokyo Station, completed in 1915. Its three main polygonal structures were arranged in a line parallel with the grid of Marunouchi's streets. From the largest, domed building in the center, a vast avenue led in stately fashion straight through Marunouchi, dividing the area exactly in half as it went, and finishing as close to the heart of the Imperial Palace as mere mortal architecture could dare to venture.

The result was, to Western eyes, merely an unusually tidy but dully derivative section of office buildings. For the Japanese, however, it was a marvelous incarnation of the values of feudalism, expressed in the vocabulary of the new age. The creation of an emperor cult had been one of the major tasks of the Meiji government; the creation of a modern economy had been another. Here in Marunouchi at the end of the period, these two tasks achieved realization in a single symbol: for lined up in immaculate dress uniform, and in the symmetrical fashion which, as the Japanese had been quick to learn, was a Western indication of order and obedience, were the offices of the mightiest of the emperor's new-style loyal retainers, the greatest business corporation in the state.

All the nineteenth-century buildings are gone from Marunouchi now—some of the replacements are already quite venerable—but that special feudalistic *frisson* can still be experienced. The symmetrical arrangement of Marunouchi's streets remains strikingly different from most other parts of the city; the rough conformity in the height of the buildings is likewise rare, and that broad avenue still leads from the palace through the marshaled bank headquarters to the old Dutch-style station, symbolic early-modern gateway to the nation.

Foreign photographers working in Tokyo rejoice in how easy it is to gain access to the roofs of all sorts of buildings around the city, even the head offices of major companies. Only in Marunouchi, it seems, is it totally impossible. Guards are on duty throughout the area, enforcing the rule that no cameras are to be pointed in the direction of the palace. It's a matter of respect; it's the bureaucratic equivalent of lowered eyes.

#

Within the traditional language of European architecture, however, the possibilities of specifically Japanese expression were extremely limited. The cultural nuances of the different elements at the architect's disposal were already well established, and they were all purely European ones. The best a Japanese could do was either, as at Marunouchi, to arrange the buildings according to a Japanese code; or else, less subtly, to slap

Kudan Kaikan (1934), an example of the prewar "crown" style.

onto the concrete or brick structure a roof that lifted orientally at the corners (they called this the "crown" style) or some other feature borrowed from the traditional vocabulary. This was the prewar way, and it was not a happy one; it was *hick*, as Mitsubishi Londontown had not been.

The leap forward came soon after the war. In Europe in the 1920s, avant-garde architects such as Le Corbusier and Walter Gropius, inspired by achievements of modern engineering such as the airplane, the suspension bridge, and the Eiffel Tower, had revolutionized ideas about what a work of architecture should look like. Their designs, reduced to the primary geometry of square and circle, were stripped of the ornaments and the historicist clichés—the arches and buttresses, frills and furbelows—which had been the boundaries of the Victorian architect's world. They lacked all allusion to the European past; chilly and severe as they often seemed, they belonged equally everywhere and nowhere.

The new architects rejected the archaic rhetoric of

Classical and Gothic, and attempted to make their buildings articulate in a way architecture had never been before. They sought to address themselves, as modern painting was also trying to do, directly to the human heart. In his book *Vers une architecture*, published in 1923, Le Corbusier put it like this:

You employ stone, wood and concrete, and with these materials you build houses and palaces; that is construction. Ingenuity is at work. But suddenly you touch my heart, you do me good, I am happy and I say: "This is beautiful." That is Architecture … walls rise towards heaven in such a way that I am moved. I perceive your intentions. Your mood has been gentle, brutal, charming or noble. The stones you have erected tell me so. You fix me to the place and my eyes regard it. They behold something which expresses a thought. A thought which reveals itself without word or sound, but solely by means of shapes which stand in a certain relationship to one another. … By the use of inert materials and starting from conditions more or less utilitarian, you have established certain relationships which have aroused my emotions. This is Architecture.

Modern architecture was born in the West and dependent for its development on Western technology, but it had had an important connection with Japan since its earliest days. Through events like the Chicago World's Fair of 1893, where the Japanese put up a traditional tea cottage and a replica of Uji City's graceful Ho-o-do, or "Phoenix Hall," and the publication in 1886 of Edward Morse's *Japanese Homes and Their Surroundings*, knowledge of the qualities of Japanese architecture spread rapidly. The last couple of decades of the nineteenth century saw a great fad for things Japanese in Europe and the United States, of which Gilbert and Sullivan's *The Mikado* and the japonesque paintings of Van Gogh and Whistler are only the most celebrated manifestations. During the same period, the strange but undeniably charming lineaments of the buildings were also steadily dripping down toward the West's creative unconscious. Frank Lloyd Wright's "prairie houses" of the 1890s and 1900s, for example, show strong and varied Japanese inspiration.

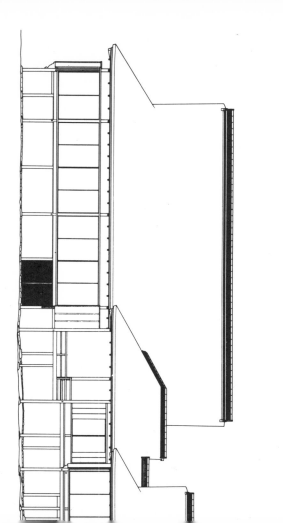

Several things about Japanese architecture were appealing. In stark contrast to Victorian neo-Gothic, it was often remarkably plain and free of decoration. Its structural principles were frankly expressed, not hidden, and the post-and-beam method of construction, though radically different from the way brick buildings were supported, was found to have analogies with building in ferroconcrete. Japanese buildings had few solid walls; with screens removed, the rooms could be flooded with light, another feature Westerners found attractive and, with the invention of plate glass and ferroconcrete, borrowable.

In contrast to the rigid symmetry of Victorian interior design, the few decorative elements admitted into a Japanese house—the *tokonoma* for example, the ceremonial alcove which resurfaced in the West in the form of Wright's monumental fireplaces—were arranged in a boldly arbitrary way which must have struck the first Westerners who saw them as reckless and eccentric. With prolonged exposure, however, the West learned to like and imitate them.

And finally there was the tatami, the thick, woven-straw block which covered the floors of all upper-class Japanese houses, and all it represented. The dimensions of the oblong tatami, roughly the size of a man, were everywhere the same, and corresponded closely to all the other dimensions of the house—even to the way land was measured, the *tsubo* unit being equivalent to two units of tatami. This remote and supposedly backward Eastern nation had developed a modular system of organizing interior and exterior space which was both rational and beautiful to a degree which the West has still not been able to match, more than a hundred years after first encountering it.

It may be possible to overstate the influence that Japan had on Europe's modern architecture, for many other avenues of inspiration were open as well. The influence, however, is very much there. In 1933, Bruno Taut, one of the German pioneers of modern architecture, visited Kyoto and was taken around the imperial villa called Katsura Rikyu, until then largely neglected by the Japanese. Katsura was a choice example of

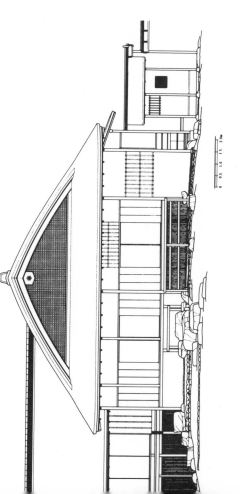

Front elevation of the main building of Katsura Rikyu, Kyoto.

146
IMAGES
OF
JAPAN

sukiya, the rustic-looking residential style favored by the Japanese aristocracy from the fifteenth century on. Sukiya-style architecture had been strongly influenced by the design of tea-ceremony cottages and Taut recognized in Katsura's spare, measured elegance a deep correspondence with what he and his colleagues were attempting thousands of miles away. He called it an "exquisite jewel." "True beauty, eternal beauty for ever inexplicable, the beauty of great art," he raved. "... In Katsura I found in a building the absolute proof of my theory, which I regarded as a valid base for modern architecture."

(Taut rejected vehemently the highly decorated and ornamented Japanese architecture typified by the Tokugawa mausoleums at Nikko, north of Tokyo. But as Japanese scholars have since pointed out, the unknown genius who designed Katsura in all probability turned his hand to the decorated style as well when the occasion demanded. Taut's dogmatic insistence on the exclusive virtue of a single style was typically European—and typical of the narrowness which was to bring modern architecture into disrepute some thirty years later.)

Taut was not alone in appreciating the worth of Katsura Rikyu. Walter Gropius wrote of it, "There is no pomp, no superfluous luxury. With great simplicity and restraint of means a truly noble edifice has been created in which a sense of freedom and peace resides as an inherent quality. No vanity, no pretentious monumentalism—but only the desire to create a balanced container for beautiful living."

The salient ideas of modern architecture crystallized at least ten years before Taut's discovery of Katsura Rikyu, so it cannot be said to have been seminal in its influence. What it did, rather, was provide a dazzlingly bright image of the Japanese aesthetic values which had been stealthily penetrating Western architectural thought for decades: hence Taut's astonishment and ecstasy. Having traveled laboriously halfway across the world, the sensation must have been uncannily like coming home.

At the same time, and in a much more methodical manner, Japanese architects continued to study

Western developments, as they had been doing diligent-ly ever since the early years of the Meiji period. The result was that when, during the '20s and '30s, the brightest of their number went to study under modern ar-chitecture's pioneers in Europe, there was infinitely more common ground than there would have been forty or even twenty years before.

The fruits of their interaction began to show up in Japan soon after the Second World War, and the man of the moment was the one Japanese architect whose name is, quite rightly, known around the world: Kenzo Tange. In Tange's work, Japanese architecture, after years of plagiarizing and fudging, suddenly found its distinctive voice. It was a voice very different from the restrained, fragile tones which readers of Taut's eulogy to Katsura Rikyu had expected to hear from the Japanese.

What Tange did was take elements of traditional Japanese design which had become part of the vocabulary pool of modern architecture and, by em-phasizing them exclusively, reinvest them with na-tionalistic significance. The most imposing of these elements was the visibly expressed structure of posts and beams. The proportions of Tange's buildings were unmistakably Japanese, too, and the overall effect was of a simple elegance which harked back to traditional aesthetics. Yet at the same time his buildings gave an impression of enormous strength and muscularity, worlds away from the delicacy of sukiya. As Reyner Banham wrote in *Age of the Masters*, published in 1962, this was the most surprising thing about them.

Kenzo Tange [has] established himself in half-a-dozen years as one of the world's outstanding architects. Tange's architec-ture, most eloquently summed up in the Town Hall he designed for Kurashiki ... is an architecture of enormous mass, fort-ress-like solidity, aggressively three-dimensional plasticity. Where the West had expected steel to be used as the equivalent of the slender wooden posts of the *Sukiya* tradition, Tange used concrete beams as the equivalent of the tree-trunk columns and thundering wooden bracketting of Japanese monumental architecture.

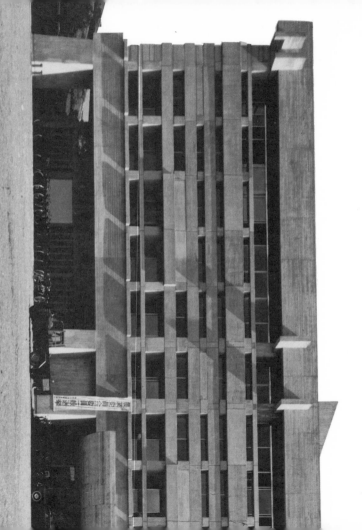

As Japan's economic recovery gathered force through the 1950s and 1960s, Tange's buildings began springing up around the country: town and city halls and culture centers. There was something deeply romantic about his work: it expressed a dream of the Japanese reborn, washed clean of the bitterness of defeat and surrender, enormously strong now, but not made ugly by strength; miraculously endowed with all the grace and spiritual nobility of the traditional ideal. The strength and the grace were not separate: the ferroconcrete which made his buildings strong also made them beautiful. This was the secret of the power of his architecture.

His best building in this period is probably the Kurashiki Town Hall mentioned by Reyner Banham, a long way from Tokyo, but the capital is dotted with buildings by other hands which bear witness to the importance of his influence. During the '50s and '60s his trademarks, particularly the use of massive concrete posts and beams and traditional proportions, became the elements of a standard "Japanese monumental" style which can still be widely seen. Tokyo's city center has several big buildings which are good examples of the safer, more conventional way his ideas were taken up. The Gallery of Eastern Antiquities at the National Museum complex in Ueno Park is typical. The concrete strength and solidity come directly from Tange, but the fact that this is a national monument leads to a more fiddly treatment of the concrete detailing, more explicitly imitative of wood. The architect, Yoshiro Taniguchi, has also given his building an *engawa*, a corridor-like space under the eaves between the columns and the plate glass, which is explicitly traditional. Altogether the building is conscientious and boring in a way that Tange, touched by Le Corbusier's genius, never allowed himself to be in this period. It also seems nationalistic in a more entrenched, less attractive way. It was in works like this that the momentum of Tange's inspiration wore itself out.

Kurashiki Town Hall.

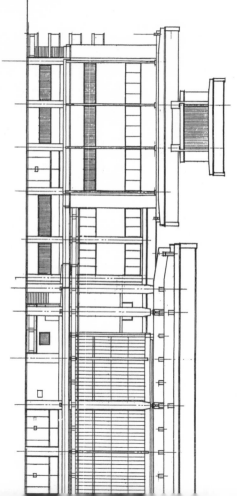

Front elevation of the Gallery of Eastern Antiquities at Ueno.

The National Theater.

Yet even with the exhaustion of that particular style, the potent idea that the aggregate of qualities described by the word "Japanese" might be expressed in the vocabulary of modern architecture remained. The hunt for new inspiration was on.

Some went right back to the roots and stayed there. In his design for the National Theater in Tokyo, for example, Hiroyuki Iwamoto took Tange's hint about traditional forms as far as it would go. It was a close replica in ferroconcrete, stained an appropriate shade of dark brown, of an eighth-century treasure repository in the ancient capital of Nara. The "log cabin"-like structure of the original, with the ends of the wall beams overlapping at the corners, was devoutly reproduced, on a greatly enlarged scale. With its long, low profile stressed by the horizontal beams, the building is undeniably elegant, but it makes one realize the greatness of what Tange did for the native style: he gave it a tongue, he let it speak. For all its monumental size, the National Theater is dumb.

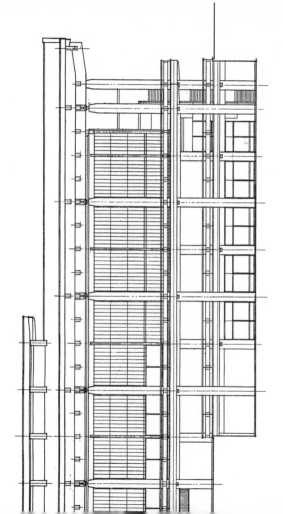

The Supreme Court.

Like Mitsubishi Londontown, the National Theater was located in the magic circle between the inner and outer moats, and directly opposite the Imperial Palace. It's here, in full view of the emperor and at the heart of the establishment, that the pressure on architects to come up with the ultimate national monument seems to be greatest. Certainly this area boasts some amazing specimens.

Kisho Kurokawa's recently completed building for the Wacoal lingerie firm, which fixes the palace with a huge, baleful, plebeian eye, is the most comical new addition to the throng. But the most extraordinary is without question Shin'ichi Okada's Supreme Court, completed in 1974. Though clearly influenced by the work of his American teacher, Paul Rudolph, Okada's court has to my knowledge no equivalent anywhere in the world.

Casting about for a way to incarnate that elusive quality called "Japanese," Okada hit on a strategy which was exactly the opposite of Tange's. Tange took the traditional elements of native design and re-created them in concrete; Okada sought out instead those properties of modern architecture which were utterly missing from the native style, and emphasized those. In particular, Okada became fascinated with solid walls. Solid walls are not a feature of traditional Japanese architecture, where posts and beams serve instead. In hot weather the front and sides of a Japanese house, made of light wood and paper, can be removed altogether. All that remain are a bunch of beams holding up a roof. The solid walls of the West's stone-and-brick buildings were one of the features that impressed the Japanese as most alien.

The Supreme Court, Okada's most famous and ambitious work, is composed, it seems, of nothing but solid walls: even the roof looks like a wall that happens to have been laid flat. Yet Okada was not out to plagiarize the West or to beat the West at its own game; he was not trying to build a contemporary Rokumeikan.

If Tange is a romantic, Okada is a mystic. Adopting an entirely and radically Western vocabulary, he steps boldly, blindly away from Japanese tradition and wades out to meet the world. Yet he remains in his heart Japanese, and if he is blind he has also in his heart this article of blind faith: that in whatever he creates, if he does it with full devotion, his Japaneseness will be manifested. By immersing himself recklessly in the tradition of the West, roving as far from home as it is possible to rove, his pure heart will seek out in that desperate extremity the essence of what it yearns for: it will create the ultimate Japanese monument.

That seems to be the mental process at work here, and it struck a responsive chord in the Japanese public at large, whose interest in modern architecture as a rule is a negative quantity. The competition through which the building's design was selected created a great stir, and Okada's was the popular favorite. The building that resulted leaves one shuddering.

Standing on a low bluff above the inner moat, it creates a world of its own—an arid, oppressive world which has no sign of life. The function of walls is to enclose space, but here they seem merely to abut other walls, and they give the impression of being monstrously thick. Furthermore there are hardly any windows—

just these great walls to be walled up in. Due to the eminence on which it stands, there is only one way to look at the court: from an inferior position up. The greenery around the base nicely sets off the building's anemic granite, but has the more significant function of hiding the ground level from view, so that all human coming and going is hidden. The structure's powerful form and the rough texture of the granite cladding give it a craggy feeling, as if it were a work of nature—to offer resistance to which would be as futile as taking a swing at the Grand Canyon.

While asserting Western spatial values with its great walls, Okada's court simultaneously denies them, for there seems to be no space within the walls and thus they are rendered absurd. Likewise, the building stands for justice—but succeeds in being a peerless symbol of authoritarianism.

Perhaps Okada's uniquely cranky strategy was a result of desperation. For ten years earlier Tange had created his own most finished expression of national personality, the two Olympic stadiums in Yoyogi Park. They have since become world-famous, though Japanese people outside the architectural profession never fail to mention the leaky roofs and the maintenance costs. Twenty years after their construction they still seem the essence of all that is healthy and sane about the great Japanese *ware-ware* ("we"), while the Supreme Court seems the essence of all that is gloomy and dangerous about it. The amazing curves of Tange's high tensile steel roofs strung between concrete masts were more than a feat of great technical daring; they conveyed a sense of Olympian suppleness, and at the same time they danced to a peculiarly Japanese tune, evoking both the sweep of the Buddhist temple roof and the seashell-like spiral of the sacred ropes of Shinto and the moat system of the Imperial Palace. This was nationalist architecture carried off with the lightest and deftest of touches.

The larger of the National Gymnasiums at Yoyogi.

As the '60s progressed, as the Olympics receded into memory and the unprecedented national boom continued, national identity ceased to be the main or only thing on the Japanese architect's mind. Economically, Japan was drawing ahead of many of the countries of Europe; this, it seemed, was to be the nation of the future, the nation of the twenty-first century. The age for importing or reinventing cathedrals seemed to be drawing to a close. The next challenge, metaphorically speaking, was the design of the Japanese moon rocket.

For a brief span of years in the late '60s and early '70s the architects of the advanced countries were in a wonderfully enjoyable state of excitement. They had managed to persuade themselves that the architect's say in the creation of the cities of the future would be enormously greater than it had ever been before. Perhaps they had been reading too much science fiction; their projections certainly resembled it. They saw themselves accorded kingly power, masterminding the construction of entire cities which, thanks to their genius, would be free of all the ills of the haphazard cities of the present.

Kenzo Tange did not start this intellectual fashion, but it was not long before he was at the center of it. What put him there was the extraordinary and visionary plan for Tokyo which he published in 1960.

Through the course of this book, plenty of mention has been made of Tokyo's varied ills and ailments: the narrow streets, the lack of order, the traffic congestion at the center, the acute shortage of living space close in. Tange proposed curing all these and more with a single dramatic stroke of architectural surgery.

The problem of congestion, he suggested reasonably, was the result of too great a concentration of activity at the center. Instead of dispersing this activity to subcenters like Shinjuku, as was to begin happening a decade later, his idea was to abolish the city's circular configuration altogether, and give it an axial one instead. He wrote:

The functions which are gathered in Tokyo seek closer mutual communication, and as a result they are drawn toward the centre of the city. This civic centre, once formed, grows larger and larger. At the same time, the people who perform the functions spread out into the suburbs in an effort to find cheap land. The city therefore assumes a form that is centripetal and radial. This has been the typical urban pattern since the middle ages, and it is the natural pattern that a city will follow if left to grow freely. . . .

In Tokyo, where movement is increasing by the day, it is urgent that a new system of transportation be constructed. And a new system which will bring city, buildings and transportation into a single organic entity is needed. . . .

We reject the concept of the metropolitan civic centre in favour of a new concept which we call the civic axis. This is tantamount to rejecting the closed organization of the centripetal pattern in favour of an open organization which makes possible a development along a linear pattern. In effect, we are proposing that the radial structure of Tokyo be replaced by an axis which develops linearly. . . .

The new axis, with its movement, would become the symbol of Tokyo's open organization and of the open society of Japan.

The hegemonic symbolism of the Imperial Palace's centrality would thus be done away with and the city's chronic congestion cured at a single stroke. In Tange's plan, mighty expressways would be driven like a knife straight through the heart of the present business center and out the other side, on piers, into Tokyo Bay. In his scheme it was the bay rather than the Shinjuku reservoir which would be the city's real *tora-no-ko*, its real precious treasure; here, potentially, was all the empty space the city needed. On a vast system of piers stretching to the far side of the bay, Tange would build a new axial heart for the city, comprising dozens of apartment complexes housed in huge structures with the same section as Mount Fuji and reminiscent of the communal thatched farmhouses found in Japan's snow country. Elsewhere there would be long, beamlike office units, schools, public spaces, shopping plazas. The whole thing would be tied together by expressways and a monorail.

Tange's plan and models were beautiful to look at, awesome to contemplate. They were the most radical

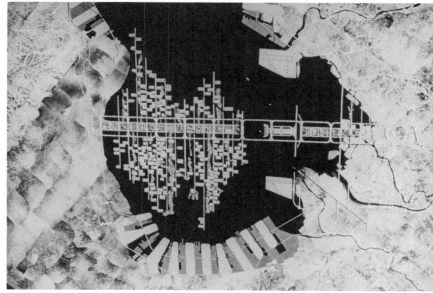

Model of Kenzo Tange's 1960 Plan for Tokyo: (*above*) aerial view; (*right*) detail showing apartment blocks at top right, elevated highway in the center, and office units.

and visionary of all megastructure projects, and made waves in architectural schools around the world. Yet, though enormously imaginative in one sense, in another they suggested an alarming failure of the imagination. Tange seemed to have forgotten that the real constitution of the city is not steel and concrete but human beings. However efficiently his plan might answer the demands of circulation, it was completely out of touch with the demands of human scale. It was way too big for anyone to relate to, quite lacking in the sort of intimacy that permits people to stay sane. Those selected to live in it would have found themselves marooned on the endless concrete of Tange's platforms, or suspended over the fetid, miso-brown waters of Tokyo Bay like monkeys in some morbid experiment. It could have turned into the biggest instant slum in the Far East.

Actually, being Japanese the residents would probably have made the best of it. Power of endurance has already been mentioned as one of the national characteristics of which the Japanese are proudest, and it's no myth. They live gracefully and long-sufferingly in the sort of public housing projects European and American tenants routinely knock to pieces. They put up with being crammed forcibly into railway cars five days a week. They would surely have put up with Tange's vast, azoic platforms, and the smell of liquid sewage in the nostrils twenty-four hours a day.

But let's thank God they didn't have to! Tange's dream of Tokyo's future was technology gone mad, technology obsessed with its own virtuosity to the extent that it quite forgot about its larger human purpose. This was one of the faults common to all the megastructural visions. The other—not perhaps a fault in vision but a fact nonetheless—was lack of realism. Only one or two of the many schemes ever got built, and even those were drastically abbreviated. The age of megastructural visions was the architectural world's last drunken fling before it woke up the next morning to find how very little change was left in its pockets.

Tange's Tokyo plan came to nothing, and he himself says it was never meant to, that it was no more than an exercise. Some of his megastructural fragments did get built, however; they still look as if they are waiting for the rest of the system to plug into them. Central Tokyo's best specimen is the Shizuoka Press and Broadcasting Center, just east of the Japanese National Railways tracks near Shimbashi Station. Like his Tokyo plan, its principle of construction is one that Tange had used many times before, one that looks, in retrospect, like his single really great idea, which he was never fully to get beyond. It's the good old post-and-beam principle. Here, as in the Tokyo plan and other of his later works, the post has swollen to enormous size and gone up in the world, too: now it's a "functional core," and contains elevators and stairs. The beams have changed, too: they have swallowed the working space which it was previously their function to support. All the other elements of the building have been disposed of; all that

Shizuoka Press and Broadcasting Center.

Sky Building No. 3.

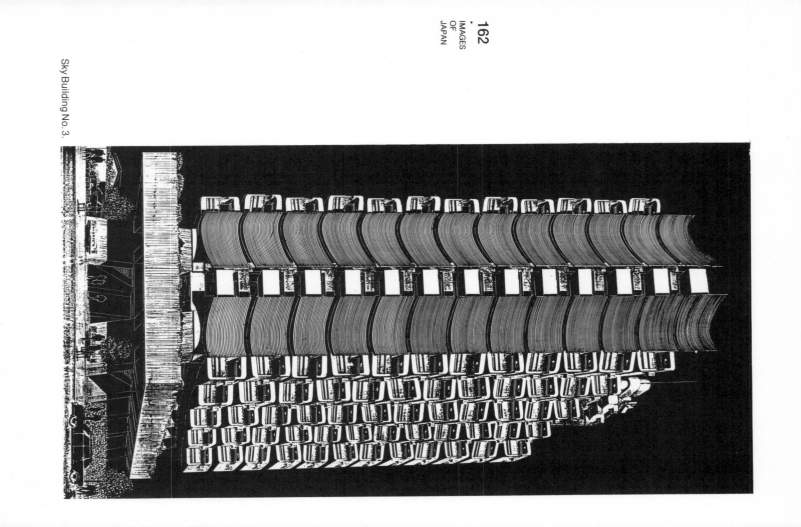

remains is a single post, notched into by a handful of vestigial beams.

As a fragment, a single unit, of the great megastructure that would obliterate the old city, it's impressive and yes, at a pinch, awesome. But the megastructure will now never be built, so the Shizuoka Building is not the beginning of something; it's the ruin of a dead idea. And in that light there's something wistful and almost comical about the way it stands there with its little stubby arms out.

Tange is not famous as a humorist, and the subversive idea occurs that this light-hearted quality was somehow smuggled into the design by a disillusioned member of his staff. In this respect the building marks an important change of mood among Japan's architects. The hopes of getting megastructures built dwindled; at the same time the suspicion that there might be something a little vulgar and unworthy about the imagination that conceived them crept in. The visionary gleam in the eye faded; the best the new architects could manage, as they scraped around for whatever work they could find, was a sardonic twinkle.

Take the Sky Building No. 3 in Shinjuku, for example, a block of flats designed by Yoji Watanabe and built in 1970. Painted silver all over, it looks as if its individual sections have been prefabricated out of aluminum and slotted together on the site. The effect is an illusion, a joke; the method of construction was in fact quite conventional. The structures on the roof are designed to look like the flight deck of an aircraft carrier: Tange's plan to go to sea may have expired, Watanabe seems to be saying, but this building is ready for anything that might be demanded of it.

As the unrealistic ambitions of the megastructure epoch were discarded, the work of imaginative architects grew cynical and fantastic, close in tone to the graphic work of people like Tsunehisa Kimura. One of Kimura's photomontages is in fact reminiscent of the Sky Building: in it, all one side of a road in the country is lined with the madly overgrown superstructures of battleships.

For what Tange and the other Japanese visionaries

had failed to take into account was the intransigence and liveliness of the city they hoped to transform. Architects were fine when they confined themselves to public buildings and national monuments. These were perhaps a necessary expense and a necessary evil in the modern age; they functioned as a flattering mirror to the state and as an image of the nation for the outside world. But they only touched the people's lives peripherally, and in extreme situations—when they'd been chosen to swim for their country in the Olympic Games, for instance, or hauled up for murder. Meanwhile life carried on, urgent, interesting, ordinary life, in the noisy shacks mentioned in the last chapter, in structures which could hardly be described as "architecture" at all with a straight face. With his Tokyo plan, Tange proposed to wrap the whole life of the city in his steely embrace. The citizens were having none of it.

For after all, planners with far more modest ambitions than Tange's could get nowhere with Tokyo. They could barely clear so much as a fire break. Expressways were introduced only by the desperate dodge of running them over the top of existing roads and canals. Shinjuku's Manhattan was made feasible by the shifting of a reservoir; if there had been people living there it could never have been contemplated. The prestidigitatory talents of a developer like Taikichiro Mori might make their mark on it, but as far as the mere planner was concerned, the city was beyond his grasp. And some of its liveliest building was beyond the architect's ken, too far beneath him to be visible at all.

The love hotels were like that—none of the architects' business. Yet, as I tried to show earlier, their development was an imaginative answer, employing all the technical skills of the modern architect, to a genuine social need. They are the loudest and most conspicuous phenomenon in what we might call the secret history of modern Japanese architecture.

The beginning of that history might somewhat arbitrarily be placed in 1911. In that year yet another of Tokyo's catastrophic fires consumed the Yoshiwara, the "nightless city," the heart of the geisha culture of old Tokyo. Afterwards some of the brothels and houses of assignation were rebuilt Western-style—sort of.

A photograph of one of the new brothels—the real thing has long since vanished—survives in the city archives. It shows that even at this early date the salient feature of the new pop architecture was well understood. Essentially the design is a dream of far away. Precision and historical accuracy are far less important than the overall effect. Some marvelous and alarming things are happening in this brothel, particularly to the cornices. The design has everything—arches, pediments, round turrets, square turrets, gas lamps, a vaulted roof. And it has these terrific cornices. One set grows upward and outward until it begins to resemble a secondary roof—or perhaps a mantlepiece, a more readily available source of inspiration. Another little cornice wraps itself neatly around the base of a square turret then races off diagonally upward, and in no time it's turned itself into the upper border of a pediment. There is more in heaven and earth, Vitruvius. . . .

Sadly, nothing of the rebuilt Yoshiwara remains for us to inspect. Even the photographic record is paltry. Elsewhere in the city there is the odd relic from early in the century, but the liveliest stuff is all postwar. Early indications of the madness to come were the extraordinary coffee shops that began to sprout up in the vicinity of college campuses in the mid-'50s: the meikyoku kissa. Like the slightly later love hotels, the gimmick was that, for the price of a cup of coffee, customers could take a lightning-fast trip to the faraway lands beyond the sea. Meikyoku kissa were extravagantly, fantastically foreign, marvelous concoctions with stained-glass windows, red brick walls lush with plastic ivy, green copper turrets, chandeliers, spiral staircases, deep-pile burgundy red carpets—and, at the heart of the illusion, the meikyoku, the classical European music, pumped at high fidelity out of monster speakers.

As more and more Japanese started traveling abroad during the '60s this sort of Brothers Grimm exoticism became too straightforward, and the anonymous artisans who designed their successors began casting their nets all over the place for inspiration. The result was a cornucopia of architectural kitsch unique in the

Charcoal grill restaurant in Shibuya.

167
IMAGES OF JAPAN

world: the tiny wooden sheds of fashionable Harajuku, painted bright pink and dispensing pancakes ... the chic coffee shops, occupying buildings ten feet wide and sixty feet high, with a lovingly applied façade of white glass tile, stainless steel, and gold paint ... the other "pencil buildings," found all over town, crammed onto tiny sites and all as busy as can be, busy being cool or raucous or svelte or effusive. There's the great one across the road from Ueno Park, again no more than twelve feet wide and eight stories high, eight identical stories of Chinese Ming elegance, with up-tilting black-tiled roofs and red-lacquered balconies on each floor. There's the brick toy shop in Ginza with windows cut like the features of a grinning face. There's the lonely charcoal grill restaurant in Shibuya that I like so much, just a dingy, mortar-faced, two-story pile with vertical slats over the upstairs window and an outdoor spiral stair-

▼ An old *meikyoku kissa,* or "classical music coffeeshop," in Ikebukuro, remodeled into a love hotel.

case going up the back, but so soulfully making the best of it with its big shabby red lantern.

A good place to get the flavor of Tokyo's pop architecture at its most concentrated is a steep, winding little alley in Shibuya called Spain Dori. It's a part of town that went its own sweet way for decades, innocent and unvisited, until a large fashion store called Parco set up in business at the top of the street. Parco was a huge success: as the first store in Tokyo to specialize in nothing but fashion, it was enormously trendy throughout the 1970s. And the little lane that is now Spain Dori woke up to find that it had become a shortcut between Parco and Shibuya Station. A man called Yasuo Uchida, who lived on the lane and had his head screwed on right, opened a little coffee shop there.

One day Mr. Uchida got it into his head to take a package holiday in Spain. Such things were just beginning to come within the reach of café proprietors. When he came back he had a wonderful idea.

He looked up and down the steep slope of higgledy-piggledy wooden houses where he lived and had his café and where his ancestors had lived for hundreds of years before him—and in a flash he saw it. It looked just like Spain. "I was only in Spain a few days," he says now, "but I visited old cities, Toledo and especially Cordoba. It was just the same—the slopes, the narrow streets." He decided to do something to make the resemblance a little more obvious.

His house was getting old anyway, and the time to rebuild was approaching, so he tore it down and replaced it with the miniature Spanish-style villa that stands there to this day. Spanish style? "Well . . . no, of course I didn't copy any actual Spanish houses," he says frankly. "After all, this isn't Spain, you know, it's Japan. I just tried to get the general Spanish feeling." And he's got it: with the thick, cake-icing-like Gaudiesque plaster on the façade, the outside steps, the arched, roofed-over verandah on the upper floor, the rococo light fixtures. The verandah gives onto a new Iberian coffee shop; Mr. Uchida's new art gallery, Spain-Zaka ["Spain Hill"] Gallery, is in the basement.

What was interesting was the reaction of the other

people on the street. They didn't report him to the local city planning office (it wouldn't have done them much good if they had). They didn't complain that he was lowering the tone of the neighborhood, or changing its historic character. Instead, they all gathered round for a good gape.

Then they went off and did likewise.

"We're all pretty close, all the people who live around here," says Mr. Uchida. "We've known each other since we were kids. There's no buying or selling of property. When I put up my new building I said to them, 'This is a challenge: you do better than this!'"

They call it Spain Dori now, "Spain Street," but it would be wrong to assume that any serious attempt has been made to give the buildings stylistic consistency, Iberian or otherwise. What has resulted, rather, is a crazily and charmingly eclectic street of noisy little cottages.

Beneath the top shop in the street, Parco's toehold here, we pass in succession two tiny stores, one of which sells buttons and perches on a corner where the track twists. Down some steps is King John, a boutique faced with red brick with a comical figure of someone like Friar Tuck pulling on a bell-rope.

After Mr. Uchida's pioneering work we reach on the left a tiny plaza let in from the lane called Shibuya Square (in English). We'd better pause here for a moment. There's quite a lot going on.

At the back of the square is a building with an English weathercock surmounting a pointed roof and, at ground floor level, a big white paper lantern advertising buckwheat noodles. In between, a painted Romeo is clambering up a *trompe l'oeil* creeper to kiss his buxom girlfriend in her Italian bedroom window.

In front of a red phone box with a complicated spike on top (Oriental, says the designer), a Spanish fountain is playing prettily beneath a Hawaiian palm tree.

A flight of dirty Greek steps goes up under a large brown beer barrel and disappears into a Japanese pub. Downstairs, to complete the round-the-world-in-fifteen-seconds tour, is a coffee shop called Café de Copain.

It sounds mad and is, but it's mad and nice, which is

Shibuya Square on Spain Dori.

what matters here. The designer of Shibuya Square is Kobo Kimura, a friendly bohemian-looking guy with graying hair hanging to his shoulders, like Mr. Uchida a Shibuya boy from way back. "It's crazy but it's not crazy," he says of the square. "It's unfinished, flawed; that's what I like. When I designed it, property in Spain Dori was still cheap, valued at about five hundred thousand yen per *tsubo*, and my budget was low, so I just tacked all the decoration and whatnot onto the old wooden row house that was already there. That was the cheapest way to do it.

"Now the property values are up to around three million yen per *tsubo* and people think the time's ripe to put up more permanent buildings. I don't agree. I'd like to keep this area flawed and temporary-looking. That way it's always capable of changing."

Throw it up, tack on some decoration, tear it down, throw up the next one, keep the costs down, the novelty up, keep the punters coming in. . . . It's little wonder the pop architects of Tokyo are on a different wavelength from the designers of supreme courts and megastructures, cathedrals, and moon rockets. It's not hard to decide which of the factions produces better architecture, conventionally judged. But neither is it hard to decide which of the two is closer to the life of the city, a closer reflection of the spirit that has rebuilt it again and again after each succeeding disaster.

The holy shrines of Ise, the most sacred buildings of the Shinto religion, are ceremonially demolished and reconstructed on adjacent sites every twenty years. Perhaps the nation's best modern monuments, "blooming unseen," are to be found among those buildings which have a comparably brief lifespan.

7

THE CITY AT THE END
OF THE WORLD

The odometer of the 1982 Triumph motorcycle reads a little over 63,000 km.

The box sidecar attached to the bike is packed with "household stuff" like sleeping bags, kitchen utensils, clothes, tools and a world map.

Taking 1 year and 10 months, Richard and Mopsa English are near the half-way mark of their around-the-world tour by motorcycle—a special tour combined with fund-raising for charity.

They are now in Japan.

[Report in the *Japan Times*, August 14, 1984]

Well, three cheers for Richard and Mopsa! You've made it just about as far as you can go. Wherever you head for next, whether it's Siberia, China, America, India, you can comfort yourself with the knowledge that you are on your way home. You've reached the outer edge. Just as in the days of Marco Polo and Francis Xavier, Japan is the last stop before the moon.

But as this is such a rich, modern country, it can be a little hard arranging that 63,000-kilometer sensation. It's all too crushingly familiar. Europeans who visit Japan tend to exclaim in disgust, "It's just like America!"

Americans tend to scowl and say, "It's just like New Jersey!" The technological surface of city life is different from that of Western countries only in the sort of detailed way that Western countries differ from one another—in the design of things like traffic lights and buses and subway-ticket machines and parking meters. Not the sort of things you feel like writing home about.

Suppose you disdain, Richard and Mopsa, the tourist biz illusionism of geisha houses and shabu-shabu parties, how can we help you best experience that frisson of distance?

I think I would take you into the station building at Shibuya, a sort of patchwork megastructure sprawling on steel legs across the center of that busy part of town. There's one window there that looks down on the square outside the station, and the big "scramble" pedestrian crossing beyond that. A scramble crossing is one where all the walk lights go green at once and stay that way for a couple of minutes. When that happens the crowds of shoppers, students, office workers, laborers, fashion models, paramilitary radicals, children, shop assistants, policemen, and layabouts who have been waiting patiently at all sides of the interchange set off at once towards the middle.

Two things are amazing and memorable about this spectacle. One is simply the numbers. The number of people who, at all hours of the day and halfway into the night, find cause to cross the road here is mind-boggling. It's a mighty tide or a plague of locusts or . . . at any rate it adds a quickening image to the bald fact that this is a city of twenty-eight million people, where twenty million people ride the trains and subways every day.

The other amazing thing is that they're all Japanese. This shouldn't be amazing because we are, after all, in Japan. But most of us in the West come from countries with large racial minorities. Japan has only very small ones. We come to Japan and find that we are an alien speck, a bobbing cork in a sea of Japanese. And our very surprise is a source of perplexity. We ought to have expected it.

Let's give that perplexity an extra twist.
Let's endow you magically with a flat in town, a TV

set, and perfect fluency in Japanese. Stay here a week or two and just soak the place up. Read all the magazines and papers, watch the box at all hours. Go out to the theater and the movies. What do you know at the end of it that you did not know before? An amazing number of miscellaneous things no doubt, among them:

The price you would need to pay for a tulip farm in Holland.

The contents of Edinburgh's military museums.

The exact state of the contemporary arts in Manhattan, with addresses, phone numbers, and descriptions of all the trendiest theaters, restaurants, clubs.

Bob Dylan's opinion about the date of the Apocalypse.

Details of all the books published about the Beatles (in English) during the past five years.

The name and biographical details of Koo Stark's new husband.

The significance and humorous intent of a new New York photographic exhibition entitled "Who Farted?" (*Onara shita no wa dare da?*).

If you went out to the theater you might have seen one or more of the following—all in Japanese, needless to say: *Cats, K2, Jesus Christ Superstar, Amadeus, The Lesson* (Ionesco), *The Ride across Lake Constance, The Architect and the Emperor of Assyria, My Fair Lady, Miss Julie,* all of which have been successfully staged during the past couple of years. *Cats* has been an enormous success, and is said by some to be better than the Broadway version. To allow it the longest possible run, a special wooden theater was built for it, in the midst of the skyscrapers in West Shinjuku.

When you stayed home you probably caught some of the eighteen American and European movies that get screened each week on the city's eight TV channels, in addition to around a dozen assorted foreign-made soaps and documentaries. You would also have seen some of the quiz programs, *Naruhodo the World!* for example, or *Sekai Marugoto How Much?,* which are among the most popular programs of all. These involve a panel of celebrities in the studio answering questions based on specially made video clips from around the world, focusing on quaint, curious, or otherwise re-markable aspects of life beyond the seas.

All this must have been pretty exhausting, but if you had turned in too early you'd have missed what many reckon to be the most interesting program on the whole Japanese TV schedule. It's on Asahi TV for an hour after midnight, seven nights a week. It's a live transmission, with simultaneous translation and Japanese anchor peo-ple to put the stuff in context, from CNN, the United States' twenty-four-hour-a-day cable news network. The show is not just the highlights, mind, not the main points of the news; it's simply a live, two-hour nightly slice of American life, including everything from the most shat-tering crimes to the most trivial fads.

A week or two after your sudden immersion in all this, you might well be in some doubt as to exactly where you are. In Asia? Europe? America? Or, as seems most like-ly, perched on a made-in-Japan satellite and hurtling over each in turn?

⌗

Cities have always been projection screens or backdrops for a very specific range of images. In one's definition of what a city is like, it is often hard to decide which is more important, the images or the backdrop. Before the twentieth century, the specificity of both was very high; fifth-century Athens was unique equally on ac-count of *Antigone* and of the Parthenon; both phe-nomena were rooted equally deeply in the city's life. In the same way, Shakespeare belonged unquestionably to London, and his achievement was in a sense the achievement of that city.

In the present age it might seem that the electronic media have eliminated this specificity, but in fact they have merely altered its nature. Thanks to those media, all the big cities in the richer countries have an enor-mously enlarged image pool, which includes a vast number of images that are to a greater or lesser extent foreign. But it's only a pool, for dipping into. Except dur-ing a world crisis or the Olympic Games, the global village remains a matter of potentiality only. The selec-tion of the images to be thrown onto the city's backdrop remains almost as much a matter of local discretion as it was in the days when most of the images themselves were home-grown.

Modern media executives as a result have awesome power. For their viewers and listeners it is they who make the world, they who decide what it is to be constituted of. Simply by emphasis and omission they can create radically different impressions of what's happening in the world, of what matters.

Every week the Japanese are fed many hours and many thousands of column inches of purely local news and information, and as this is a country where dramatic or violent events are remarkably rare, much of this is trivial in the extreme. Yet besides this they are also inundated with information about the outside world in a quantity which must be unique in history. More books are translated into Japanese than into any other language. Big American films open days or weeks after New York. West End and Broadway hits are translated and staged within months of attaining success. The curious Tokyoite can, without mastering a sentence of English, acquire an extraordinary intimacy with the contemporary culture of the West.

By contrast the American or European learns next to nothing about Japan. He hears about trade frictions, summit meetings; the odd Japanese oddity may make it through the wires, providing it's odd enough: phallic festivals, train-pushers, in-taxi *karaoke*, "robot murders factory worker." Rumors of Japanese success and prosperity lour like thunder clouds. Opportunistic politicians hurl statistics about Japanese unions or unemployment at their opponents like poisoned darts. The picture is ill-defined; it's all vaguely ghastly and incredible.

Japan is an occasional brightly colored irritation in the West's eye. Japan's eyes, on the other hand, are trained steadily on the West practically twenty-four hours a day.

One of the consequences of this is that the distance between Japan and the West, psychologically speaking, is much smaller than that between the West and Japan. Japanese people, not only businessmen but office girls, students, farmers, and housewives and grandmothers, fly around the world with extraordinary blitheness these days. They know all about what to expect at the other end; the images have been raining down on them for years. They do it almost as casually as they would catch a bus. Hiroaki Sato, a translator and long-term resident of New York, has noticed the change. "In the early '70s," he wrote in his column in the *Mainichi Daily News*, "an American describing Japanese in New York never forgot to point out that these Orientals were easy to spot: they invariably went about in groups, solemnly attired in dark business suits." Not any more; when two of Sato's friends arrived recently from the old country for a first visit, he was bemused to notice that they had come wearing rubber slippers. Meanwhile the odd bold Western adventurers struggle ashore at Narita, like Richard and Mopsa, usually with only the haziest idea of what awaits them, and usually on their way around the world. It's almost the only admissible pretext for coming such a frightful long way, to the very end of the earth.

＃

Japan, bitterly conscious of being peripheral ever since it learned it was not alone in the world, now struggles to make itself a new center. The nation fills up its eyes and ears with the latest pictures and noises of the great world, fills its mouth with thousands of English words. Tokyo fills up with emblems of the alien values that have been embraced, the Rokumeikan, the Imperial Hotel, the skyscrapers of Shinjuku. More and more the ambition of "catching up" is realized. Japan becomes a center of manufacturing, of finance, of import and export. Japan becomes as central in hard economic fact as it is in cultural aspiration. The seas that once divided now unite. The world map demands to be redrawn, with Tokyo, the unquestionably preeminent city, bang in the middle of it.

Only the funny thing is, hardly anybody in the world knows it, hardly anybody will admit it. All eyes are fixed on New York or Paris, those dying cities. People await the rousing from its slumber of Beijing, the apotheosis of Buenos Aires or Seoul. Japan is no sooner called "number one" by a Harvard professor than its downfall is discussed. Its economic hegemony is disguised in products so brilliantly adapted to the Western environments in which they must sell that they melt instantly into people's lives. They bear names which are calculatedly neutral—Pioneer, Panasonic, Sony—or sell instead under the cover of American or European brand names.

The main discipline learned by Japanese children is self-effacement, and Japan goes along with the Western insistence that it is still not really a place that matters very much. The *honne*, the actual facts of Japanese strength, are well understood by all parties, and are the basis for discussion when Nissan or Honda contemplate building plants abroad, or when international economic or technological pacts are discussed. But the *tatemae*, the comfortable fiction generally agreed on, is that Japan is still out at the edge of things. Thus are Western feathers smoothed, Western vanities appeased; thus does Japan continue to learn more and more about the West, while the West continues to get by with knowing the bare minimum about Japan.

For the West this is much the least distressing way to get along with Japan's new power. But it is also the West's guarantee of eventual oblivion. This is well on the way to coming about. And the more desperate things become, the more energy is thrown into maintaining the illusion that the status quo is unchanged.

A new realism is required in the West's attitude to Japan, and if it is ever achieved it will be a turning point in Western history. It will be the beginning of the end of the deeply ingrained habit of imperialism. In 1961 the philosopher Paul Ricouer wrote,

No-one can say what will become of our civilization when it has really met different civilizations by means other than the shock of conquest and domination. But we have to admit that this encounter has not yet taken place at the level of an authentic dialogue. That is why we are in a kind of lull or interregnum in which we can no longer practice the dogmatism of a single truth and in which we are not yet capable of conquering the scepticism into which we have stepped. We are in a tunnel, at the twilight of dogmatism and the dawn of real dialogues.

Japan, whose civilization now challenges the West's, has attained that position by just such a willingness to talk, to learn, to entertain alien notions. As a result of more than a hundred years of effort, Japan's best minds can now draw on Western ideas and traditions as freely as they can on Japanese ones. The architect Arata Isozaki put it like this:

As I can understand Japanese and am able to read even quite difficult texts, Japanese classic buildings such as Katsura Rikyu and the shrines at Ise are of course accessible to me. But my generation is the first which has been able to look at, for example, the Parthenon, Chartres and the works of Palladio in the same way as we look at Japanese classics, and from the same distance. It's my generation's good fortune that we are able to learn from this situation.

⚌

Just suppose that some of the Westerners who come to Tokyo made that vertiginous and humiliating leap from the mentality of teacher to that of learner. Could this metropolis have anything at all to tell them?

If the answer is a tentative "yes," it is not something that is going to come about easily. Whatever impressions he takes away of Japan in general, the foreign visitor's opinion of Tokyo is more than likely to be very negative. In the old days he would have given it the most perfunctory of once-overs before heading down to "Kyoto the Beautiful." Recently he tends to linger, snagged by such attractions as Tokyo Disneyland and the bargain electronics center at Akihabara. He may also encounter one of the new English-language guides to the city which have appeared in swift succession in the past couple of years, all of them written by knowledgeable fans of the city, all of them urging the passer-through to accept that, despite indications to the contrary, Tokyo really is one hell of a place.

The tourist reads the guides, takes the tours, explores a bit on his own, and doesn't believe a word of it. He prefers to believe instead the evidence provided by his own senses. He finds himself in a city of mind-boggling ugliness; a city with almost nothing of beauty to show for its nearly four hundred years of history; a city whose gummed-up roads and random dispersal of homes, shops, offices, and factories bear eloquent testimony to the folly of putting up a vast urban complex without even the embryo of a plan.

All the tourist's observations are correct, and having made them he will likely pile into the bullet train for Kyoto as quickly as he can, cursing authors such as the present one for wasting his time as he does so.

Alternatively he could stick around a bit longer. For although he has truly seen one aspect of Tokyo's reality, he has not grasped the whole story. And at the far side of the unpleasant truths he has identified could well lie the start of one of the "real dialogues" spoken of by Paul Ricouer.

Perhaps the fundamental reason for Tokyo's ugliness is that it lacks all integration. The charms of the traditional Western city—vistas, squares, crescents, and the sense of a controlling intelligence behind such forms—are entirely absent. Instead there is an anarchic concrete jumble. In place of the delicate sense of order found in the West is the blunt legalistic instrument of volume restrictions that causes buildings to be sliced to shape much in the way a butcher dresses meat.

Yet the city's lack of integration, one gradually comes to realize, is not a hideous mistake, not a story of virtuous intentions steamrollered by greed. It is rather that the sense of integration itself is an alien concept, a sort of beauty which the Japanese do not look to find. In its place is a concern for and an attachment to particular buildings and spaces in the city taken one at a time, with their particular qualities of composure, style, wit, or charm. Each is enjoyed on its own merits; the viewer then takes a breath of air, metaphorically speaking, and shifts his attention to the next one.

This is the way the Japanese have enjoyed buildings and the spaces around and between them for centuries. The design of a sprawling complex such as Katsura Rikyu shows the same qualities. Unlike the stately homes of England, Katsura was never intended to be appreciated from a stationary viewpoint. Only by moving through it, taking in its constantly shifting sequence of

Noa Building.

views and environments, can the visitor truly enjoy it.

Both Katsura and Tokyo (and Kyoto, too, for that matter) thus take time and patience to appreciate. They require suspension of the desire to know and judge everything all at once, a willingness to linger, to be taken by surprise. Affluence has not brought Tokyo any closer to the Western ideal of urban beauty, but it has resulted in a proliferation of its charming surprises. Anybody wanting to check the point might like to take a stroll in the backstreets of an area such as Harajuku or Akasaka, or residential Sendagaya. The number of gay, daring, nutty, natty little dwellings, offices, and shops which have gone up in the past decade is extraordinary. This is the species of urban beauty at which Tokyo is able to excel, and it is one to which these times are well suited. Whether we account it a good or bad thing, it's a fact that the characteristic product of modern architecture is the single, discrete building, the once-and-for-all embodiment of individual vision, standing out boldly from its environment. What modern architecture has not succeeded in doing is creating a vernacular with anything approaching the elegance, versatility, or popularity of, say, the Georgian style which beautified large swaths of England's towns and cities in the eighteenth and early nineteenth centuries.

This failure has been bad news for the integrative cities of the West. It has broken their long vistas, spoiled their harmonies, weighed them down with bitterly parodic versions of the old vernacular like the English semi-detached and the housing project. But it's a failure which has not touched Tokyo at all, as there was nothing to damage in this way. What has happened instead is that the individualistic bias of modern architecture has multiplied Tokyo's charming surprises a thousandfold.

It has resulted in the odd enigmatic masterpiece, too, like Seiichi Shirai's Noa Building, the original "dark tower," a sleek black lipstick-holder emerging from a massive red brick plinth on a slight eminence that is also a major crossroads, just up the street from Taikichiro Mori's stronghold in Toranomon.

As a symbol of all that is exciting and splendid about Tokyo's architecture, the Noa Building is without peers. The great achievement of the Western architectural tradition has been the creation of an atmosphere of rocklike security from which all ambiguity is rigorously banished. A work like the Noa Building has almost the opposite effect. Its presence, as one walks up the steep hill towards it, is both so commanding and so mysterious that it throws all assumptions about the city that surrounds it into doubt. It occupies the strategic site in the locality with superb authority—but authority deriving from where? Noa offers no answers.

It's in the midst of just such doubt and confusion that the creativity of contemporary Tokyo thrives. The Japanese had too much certainty for far too long.

Disruption since the war has rocked their society but has helped set their imaginations free. Back in the late 1950s, at the height of his powers, Kenzo Tange wrote:

Until only very recently, Japan was constantly under the control of an absolute state, and the cultural energy of the people as a whole—the energy with which they might have created new forms—was confined and suppressed. This was especially true in the Tokugawa period, when the government strove relentlessly to prevent social change. Only in our own times has the energy of which I speak begun to be released. It is still working in a confused medium, and much remains to be done before real order is achieved, but it is certain that this energy will do much to convert Japanese tradition into something new and creative.

Tange's "order" remains elusive, but his prediction was sound. The level of creativity—particularly in fields such as fashion, design, and architecture—has indeed soared.

⊹

Western cities, and particularly European cities, seem cast as the permanent fall-guys of the modern world: everything it does causes them grief. New buildings smash their historic patterns, highways tie them in knots, suburbs destroy their cohesion. It's one long sob story after another.

Tokyo, though badly congested and polluted, seems on the other hand to possess some deep affinity with the trend of the times. As I have suggested, modern architecture (at its best) does not blight modern Tokyo; it gives it charm, it sets it free. Similarly the terrific pace of change does not leave Tokyo moaning in bewilderment about vanished monuments and landmarks. Its long apprenticeship in coping with fire and earthquake has left it with a terrific insouciance in the face of change. The appearance of neighborhoods may be transformed dramatically from one week to the next. Charming old corners disappear, memories go up in smoke, but in compensation there is no dereliction, there are no abandoned sections festering away. The city's most notorious "ghetto," Sanya, a section full of flophouses for day-laborers, is so clean and neat (with the exception of the odd drunk full length on the road) that it looks like something out of Disneyland.

Everything changes, everything is torn down and thrown up again five stories higher, with complete lack of sentimentality, and almost complete indifference (except when there's an architect on the payroll) to what the finished result may look like. But at the same time, some things hardly change at all. No one slaps conservation orders on them or gets up petitions, yet some aspects of the city carry on very much as they have done ever since people started living there.

These traditions are not what Westerners tend to think of as city things because they are related to nature and to the wheeling of the seasons, phenomena to which the city air is customarily thought noxious. Tokyo's people, though, have never found any difficulty in welcoming them in, and making their observation an intrinsic part of city life. This remains almost as true today as it was a hundred years ago. Tokyoites troop out to view the city's rare snowfalls, the plum blossom, and the cherry blossom, they clog the streets for summer festivals where they execute decorous dances for the entertainment of the dead. In autumn they admire the harvest moon, at New Year's they crowd the shrines. The year is full of such events. As Edward G. Seidensticker has put it,

[Tokyo] remained close to nature as has no other great city in the world. In midsummer, for the festival of the dead, people returned in huge numbers to their villages, and those who could not go had village dances in the city. It was the double life at its best. Civilization and Enlightenment had to come, perhaps, but they did not require giving up the old sense of the earth.

Perhaps in some unquantifiable manner it is this "sense of the earth," this almost rustic rootedness (they put far more value on land than buildings) that is behind the heroic resilience of the people of Tokyo. It may be their closeness to the psychology of the farmer, with his resignation to the cycles of the seasons and the vagaries of the elements, that has helped them stay sane in the face of everything.

Several years ago one of Japan's most celebrated avant-garde theater directors, Tadashi Suzuki, staged a production of Euripides' *The Trojan Women* that drew an analogy between the sufferings of Troy's women and those of the women of Japan, surviving amid the ashes of their cities at the end of the last war. It was a treatment which made for a powerful contemporary drama, but as an analogy it had one important limitation: Troy burned down and stayed down until its ruins were dug up by modern archeologists. Tokyo burned down and was almost immediately thrown right back up again, just as it had been countless times before. Suzuki's Tokyo woman howls and roars her grief at proper Euripidean length; the real thing, bitterly mortified though she surely was, barely took time to draw breath before going back again to the business of living.

"And for all this," as Gerard Manley Hopkins wrote in another context, "nature is never spent; / There lives the dearest freshness deep down things." However artificial and sophisticated the city's life becomes, something fundamental in it remains beyond the reach of flames and temblors. Each time they put the town together again it is still Tokyo.

Is there something here the world could learn from?

‡

A day or two after I put the final full stop to the above, the sixty-first anniversary of Tokyo's greatest earthquake was marked in eastern Japan by antidisaster drills in which, according to press reports, some fourteen million people took part. A TV documentary on the possible consequences for the capital of another great earthquake was broadcast. A ridiculous old *Towering Inferno*-type feature film on the same topic was screened. A private seismologist predicted that as many as three million could die next time around.

Meanwhile in towns in the Izu Peninsula, sixty miles south of Tokyo, shopkeepers were doing a tremendous trade in canned food and drinking water, emergency antiearthquake equipment, bags for keeping valuables safe, and devices for preventing furniture from falling over. There was nothing superstitious about the shopping spree: the Meteorological Agency recorded 2,931 tremors in the Izu area between August 30 and September 7, including 61 strong enough to be sensed by human beings. On one day alone, September 5, there were 790 recorded jolts.

When the next big earthquake came, however, a mere week later, it was from an unexpected direction. I had just left the house with my boy shortly before nine in the morning, and might not have noticed anything but for the rattling of nearby windows. Then the phone rang and I went back inside to answer it. It was a badly shaken up friend forty miles away, calling to check that we were OK.

We were fine and so was Tokyo, though the city's buildings swayed for half a minute. A mountain village called Otakimura, however, 100-odd miles west of the capital, was a mess. The epicenter of the quake was right underneath it. Mudslides carried homes down the steep slopes, burying more than twenty people alive, destroying the roads and electric and telephone wires. For days afterward the survivors sheltering in a local school got little sleep as aftershocks continued.

A few days after that big one I woke early in the morning with the house tipping backward and forward again and sat up to wait till it finished. Then I wrote in my diary what it felt like.

It starts in the windows, rattling.
You know it's not wind because it's regular, rhythmical.
It goes straight away as heat to your hands and feet, as tension to your shoulders.
The rhythm, the regularity is what's amazing, to be part of that beat.

Our kid snored through the whole performance. I turned off the light and went back to sleep.

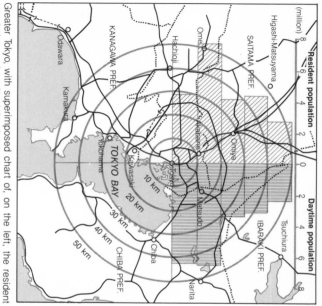

Greater Tokyo, with superimposed chart of, on the left, the resident population, and on the right, the daytime population, according to the distance from the center.

Central Tokyo.

BIBLIOGRAPHY

This book is based in part on interviews with the following people, conducted between 1982 and 1985: Takamitsu Azuma, Hiromichi Ishizuka, and Nobuo Marui of Tokyo Municipal University's Toshi Kenkyu Center. Arata Isozaki; Masao Itagaki, and Jun'ichi Seto of *Mainichi Shimbun*, Kobo Kimura, Tsunehisa Kimura, Professor Fumihiko Maki of Tokyo University, Taikichiro Mori, Yoshitaro Muramatsu, Nagisa Oshima, Professor Edward G. Seidensticker, Takashi Suzuki, Minoru Takeyama, and Yasuo Uchida. Details of sources quoted in the text are as follows:

Banham, Reyner. *Age of the Masters.* New York: Harper and Row, 1962.

Bazin, Germain. *The Baroque: Principles, Styles, Modes, Themes.* New York: Norton, 1978.

Calvino, Italo. *Invisible Cities.* Translated by William Weaver. New York: Harcourt Brace Jovanovich, 1974.

Earthquake Disaster Prediction Research Group of the Metropolitan Research Center. *Thinking about Earthquake Disasters* (in Japanese). Tokyo: Tokyo Municipal University, 1983.

Eastham, Todd R. "There's No Breaking This Chain of Love." UPI Report in *Japan Times Weekly,* February 5, 1983.

Futagawa, Yukio. Interview with Arata Isozaki. Translated by Peter Popham. *GA Document 8* (October 1983): 8.

Gropius, Walter, and Kenzo Tange. *Katsura: Tradition and Creation in Japanese Architecture.* New Haven: Yale University Press, 1960.

Ishii, Kazuhiro. "Urban Beauty in Tokyo." *Japan Architect,* April 1982.

Jacobs, Jane. *The Death and Life of Great American Cities.* New York: Random House, 1961.

Kurokawa, Kisho. *Metabolism in Architecture.* London: Studio Vista, 1977.

Le Corbusier (C. E. Jeanneret). *Towards a New Architecture.* 1973. English-language edition of *Vers une architecture* Cited in *Modern Architecture: A Critical History,* by Kenneth Frampton. New York and Toronto: Oxford University Press, 1980.

Mumford, Lewis. *The City in History.* London: Secker and Warburg, 1961.

Nagasawa, Kiyoshi. Interview with Arata Isozaki. *Playboy* (Japanese-language edition), April 1984.

Nakane, Chie. *Japanese Society.* Berkeley: University of California Press, 1970.

Nakano, Ann. "If Karaoke Be the Food of Love . . ." *Mainichi Daily News,* February 1, 1980.

Ricoeur, Paul. *History and Truth.* (Illinois:Northwestern University Press, 1961). Cited in "Prospects for a Critical Regionalism," by Kenneth Frampton. *Yale Architectural Journal* 20 (1983).

Seidensticker, Edward. *Low City, High City.* New York: Alfred A. Knopf, 1983.

Shinjuku New Business Center Public Construction Corporation. *Construction of the Shinjuku New Business Center.* Tokyo, May 1968.

Tange, Kenzo. "A Plan for Tokyo—1960—Toward a Structural Reorganization." *SD,* January 1980.

Taut, Bruno. *Houses and People of Japan.* Tokyo: Sanseido Press, 1937.

Toynbee, Polly. "Soka Gakkai and the Toynbee 'Endorsement,'" *Daily Yomiuri,* May 27, 1984.

定価2,980円
in Japan